Make Confident Decisions

Karen Mannering

I would like to dedicate this book to all my friends, colleagues and teams I have worked with over the years.

I would also love to thank Liz Pilcher for all her help and support during the writing of this book.

Make Confident Decisions

Karen Mannering

Hodder Education

338 Euston Road, London NW1 3BH

Hodder Education is an Hachette UK company

First published in UK 2012 by Hodder Education

First published in US 2012 by The McGraw-Hill Companies, Inc.

Copyright © 2012 Karen Mannering

British Library Cataloguing in Publication Data: a catalogue record
for this title is available from the British Library.

Library of Congress Catalog Card Number: on file.

10 9 8 7 6 5 4 3 2 1

The publisher has used its best endeavours to ensure that any
website addresses referred to in this book are correct and active at
the time of going to press. However, the publisher and the author
have no responsibility for the websites and can make no guarantee
that a site will remain live or that the content will remain relevant,
decent or appropriate.

The publisher has made every effort to mark as such all words
which it believes to be trademarks. The publisher should also
like to make it clear that the presence of a word in the book,
whether marked or unmarked, in no way affects its legal status as
a trademark.

Every reasonable effort has been made by the publisher to trace the
copyright holders of material in this book. Any errors or omissions
should be notified in writing to the publisher, who will endeavour
to rectify the situation for any reprints and future editions.

Hachette UK's policy is to use papers that are natural, renewable
and recyclable products and made from wood grown in sustainable
forests. The logging and manufacturing processes are expected to
conform to the environmental regulations of the country of origin.

www.hoddereducation.co.uk

Cover image © Ioannis Pantziaras – Fotalia

Typeset by Cenveo Publisher Services

Printed and bound by CPI Group (UK) Ltd, Croydon, CR0 4YY

Also available
in ebook

Contents

Meet the author   ix
Introduction   x

1   How we make decisions   1
    Self-assessment   1
    Our conscious versus our unconscious brain   3
    Making connections   4
    The benefit of allowing enough time   6
    Decision blockers   7
    The rollercoaster effect   9
    Working with your energy   9
    Losing the guilt   11
    Focus points   11
    Case studies   12
    Next step   12
2   Developing the right skills   13
    Self-assessment   13
    The decision-making process   15
    Focus points   25
    Case studies   26
    Next step   26
3   Generating more ideas and options   27
    Self-assessment   27
    How creative do you need to be?   30
    No man is an island   31
    Unrelated objects   32
    Doodle doo   33
    Music maestro   34
    Kinaesthetic challenge   34
    Brainstorming   35
    Adopt a questioning approach   37
    Sleep on it   37
    Narrow your options   38
    Focus points   39

	Case studies	39
	Next step	40
4	**Managing risk**	**41**
	Self-assessment	41
	What is risk?	43
	Why is calculating risk important?	44
	What do we need to consider?	45
	Project-focused risk	46
	Security-focused risk	47
	Safety-focused risk	48
	Contingencies	49
	Using the traffic light system	51
	Making your decision based on risk	52
	Focus points	53
	Case studies	54
	Next step	55
5	**Intuitive or rash?**	**56**
	Self-assessment	56
	The mystery of decision making	58
	When and how to make a fast decision	60
	Tapping into your senses	62
	Unconscious intelligence	63
	Going with the group	64
	Your moral compass	65
	If it all goes wrong...	66
	Focus points	67
	Case studies	67
	Next step	68
6	**Structured decision making**	**69**
	Self-assessment	69
	Why get caught up in structure?	71
	The beautiful decision	72
	Going for consensus	74
	Focus groups	75
	Introducing a simple grid	76
	Feeling the weight	78
	A game of consequences	80
	Winners and losers	81

	Making it happen	82
	Focus points	83
	Case studies	83
	Next step	84
7	**Business-related decisions**	**85**
	Self-assessment	85
	Business strategy and decision making	87
	Operational decisions	89
	Decisions in meetings	90
	Negotiating decisions	91
	Decision making and teams	92
	Recruitment decisions	93
	Appraisal decisions	95
	Developing others to make decisions	96
	Delegating decisions	97
	Focus points	97
	Case studies	98
	Next step	99
8	**Decisions clouded by emotions**	**100**
	Self-assessment	100
	What is going on?	102
	Dealing with family decisions	103
	Decisions with children	104
	The expectancy effect	106
	Stereotyping	107
	Halo and horns	108
	Negative bias	109
	Power differences	110
	Focus points	111
	Case studies	112
	Next step	112
9	**Life-changing decisions**	**113**
	Self-assessment	113
	Serendipity: chance or a great decision?	115
	Choosing (or losing) a partner	117
	Selecting a school or university	118
	Where to live?	119
	Changing work or career	121

Deciding when relatives need care   122
Deciding to start a family   123
Deciding to take a career break   123
Deciding the rest of your life   125
Focus points   126
Case studies   126
Next step   127

10 Beyond the decisions   128
Self-assessment   128
The tombstone shocker   130
Volunteering   131
The legacy of change and rebirth   132
Deciding to create a lasting memory   132
Where there's a will...   134
A last-minute decision to marry   135
Pets   136
Decisions around money   136
Deciding to donate your organs   137
Communication is the key   137
Focus points   138
Case studies   139
Next step   139

Taking it further   140
Helpful websites   140
Further reading   140
Contacts   141
Index   142

Meet the author

A world without decisions is just impossible. Everywhere we turn there are decisions to make, from the smallest – such as which sock to put on first in the morning – to the most life-changing – such as who to marry and whether to take on a mortgage.

Throughout my life I have had to make many decisions, both at work and in my private life, and I believe that there are ways of making decisions that take the sting out of our biggest fear: what if we make the wrong decision?

I have been delivering most of the techniques explained in this book through my training programmes and seminars for developing people, and I would now like to share them with you. These techniques will enable you to make quality decisions confidently, in a whole range of situations. By working through this book, you will be able to look critically at the different types of decision you need to make, what the impact of a decision might be, and how to apply the right technique in order to come to a decision in a timely way.

There are also numerous tips and tricks in every chapter that can save you time and energy; facing a decision can often turn people into procrastinators, and time hovering over the 'right' answer can be time wasted. You will also learn through the case studies that follow two characters, Chris and Pat, as they make major decisions in their lives.

Karen Mannering, 2012

Introduction

Decisions, decisions! The need to make them is constant, and they surround us in all their various forms throughout our life. How do we decide what to wear? Who to invite? How to spend our money? How much to give to charity? What to invest in? Should we start up that business during a recession? Should we sell up and move? It's no wonder that so many of us end up with 'decision paralysis', where we are so scared of making a decision that we make no decision at all.

Decisions are everywhere in our lives and are a normal part of our every day. Some will be larger than others, some will affect only you, and others may affect many hundreds of people. Avoiding them is not only fruitless but nigh on impossible. How fantastic, then, that we can all learn to make decisions in a number of ways that enable us to cope better with our lives.

Here are some 'rules', or truths, about decision making that are worth remembering as you read this book:

1 Avoiding a decision is taking the decision not to act

Many us have heard stories of near misses or 'if onlys', where someone lost the opportunity of a lifetime because they did not act quickly or decisively enough. For many others, the fear of making the wrong decision leads them to take no action at all. And yet taking no action is a decision, too – a decision to step back and allow whatever happens to happen. So, let's kill the first assumption that so many people make – that avoiding decisions means never having to make them.

2 Everyone makes decisions, at all levels in the organization

People often tell me that they believe effective decision making is something that managers do. Many times I have heard people say things like, 'I am only a support worker and so I am not paid to make decisions,' but they are wrong. They may not be making decisions at a strategic level but they are still making decisions all the time. You may not be the person who decides whether your company should open a new office in Finland, but you still have a role in making decisions at work at your own specific level.

3 Decision making is not a skill you are blessed with: it can be learned

Yes, decision making is a key skill for managers, but it is also a key skill for life. At this point you may be thinking, 'Well, I am just not blessed with this great decision-making ability.' Well, did you decide what to wear this morning? Did you decide what to have for breakfast? How to get to work? Whether to pick up a coffee on the way? Latte or cappuccino? These are the kinds of decision we all make every day, so we all have this ability. What you probably mean is that you feel you don't have the skill to make complex decisions confidently.

4 The biggest decisions we make have nothing to do with work

'OK,' you may say, 'but these are small examples. I would never feel confident enough to make the huge decisions that I hear about at work.' This is to forget that three of the biggest (and most expensive) decisions we will ever make are choosing a place to live, choosing a life partner and deciding whether to start a family. The decisions you make in these three areas will have an impact on your whole life and will affect your finances accordingly, and yet none of them are 'work' decisions.

5 Be bold! Work with the information you have, and forge ahead

The biggest cause of decision paralysis is the fear of making the wrong decision. However, in most situations you will never know what might have happened if you had decided to take the other option. For example, imagine you were choosing between two properties to buy and, after much deliberating, you decide on one and opt for that. There is no point agonizing over whether you made the right choice because you will never know how your life would have turned out had you chosen the other one. Perhaps, if you had waited a little longer, a third option would have appeared on the market. You will never know, and therefore whether you have made the right decision or not remains a moot point. Further, when we later judge whether that decision was great or poor, we are often doing so in hindsight when we already know the outcome. To say that you should have known this in advance is being too hard on yourself as you made the decision based on the information you had at the time.

6 You can learn techniques to become a better decision maker

When I began researching this book on decision making, I wanted to demonstrate a number of techniques that *anyone* can use when getting to grips with decision making. We will start by looking at how decisions are made, the skills you need to become a proficient decision maker, how you can increase the number of options at your disposal and why you need to be aware of the amount of risk. There is a time and place for intuitive decision making in addition to carefully considered decisions, and these will be discussed, along with a number of business-related decisions.

Towards the end of this book, we will be looking at how emotions can affect your decision making and how they can interfere with our logical thoughts. We need to be aware of this because some decisions are literally life changing, and we may not be using the best method for making them. Finally, there are some decisions we may make that will have an impact beyond our own lifetime, and have implications for others. My hope is that by the end of this book you will have a good range of tips and techniques for confronting the huge range of decisions you will make throughout your life, and that you are able to make those decisions with confidence.

Author's note

Throughout this book there are boxes containing activities or key points that are designed to help you in various ways:

Try it now: these feature short activities that enable you either to prepare for the next section or to consolidate your learning. They will also enable you to create your own examples and help make the book more relevant to your own life.

Remember this: these are key points that are useful to remember.

Key ideas: these are important concepts or ideas to consider, which you can apply to your life.

Focus points: found at the end of each chapter, these will help you to carry away the key learning points from what you have just read.

Case studies: throughout this book we will be following Chris and Pat in their quest to be better at making decisions.

You may also decide to dip in and out of the book rather than read it from start to finish, concentrating on the subjects that seem most relevant to you or that you feel need more of your attention. As you start using some of the techniques, you might also like to record your experiences in note form, so that you can reflect on how you made each decision and whether the outcome was as expected.

1

How we make decisions

Goal: To investigate how we currently make decisions and whether our techniques are working in every aspect of our lives.

Self-assessment

Read the following statements about making decisions, and say how much you agree with them by circling one of the numbers. If you disagree with the statement circle the 1, if you neither agree nor disagree circle the 3, and if you fully agree circle the 5:

I enjoy making decisions	1 2 3 4 5
I feel I make good decisions	1 2 3 4 5
I am happy and confident when I'm asked to make a decision	1 2 3 4 5
I don't mind when a friend or partner asks me to make a decision	1 2 3 4 5
I feel I am consistent in how I make decisions	1 2 3 4 5
I understand completely how I make decisions	1 2 3 4 5
I am aware of several techniques that I use in my decision making	1 2 3 4 5
I prefer making smaller decisions to large ones	1 2 3 4 5
I try to avoid making decisions if I can	1 2 3 4 5
My decision-making techniques are holding me back	1 2 3 4 5

Now add up your score and put the total in the box. **Total score =**

Score	Result
41–50	You are confident in your ability to make decisions, but you can still benefit from this book by either revisiting your skills or considering whether there are better methods available. You may only need to dip into certain sections of this book, but try to undertake each activity in the sections you choose as they will enhance your learning and enable you to put the points into context.
26–40	You are confident about making some decisions in some situations. Reading this book will enable you to build on this and enhance the skills you already have, in addition to offering you more ideas and techniques. You also need to consider the activities carefully, and after trying some of the techniques, reflect on their usefulness.
Below 25	You lack confidence in decision making, and this book will take you on a journey where you can learn to make good-quality decisions in addition to building your confidence. Consider keeping a 'decision diary' so that you can see how you progress as you move through the book.

How do you make a decision? Do you write everything down, go with your 'gut feeling' or play a childhood game like 'eeny, meeny miney mo' or 'ip, dip, doo' to deselect the other options until you are left with a clear contender? I am sure you see that some of these options are a little haphazard and others inappropriate, so why do we resort to these methods? Why is it so difficult to make a decision?

As we progress throughout this book it will be helpful to have some paper and a pencil or pen to hand. This is so that you can make notes as you go along and also carry out the exercises as they occur throughout the book.

Our conscious versus our unconscious brain

Do we make decisions consciously or not? The answer is that it depends on the type of decision we are making. In many aspects of our lives, our decision making is unconscious, and with good reason. For example, if you had to complete a decision chart every morning to decide which was the best route to take to work, by the time you had analysed the results you would probably be late anyway. It's the same with choosing what to eat for breakfast. So many of our everyday activities include decisions that need to be made regularly, and many of them are taken care of by our unconscious selector.

However, some of our everyday decisions are not automatic, such as deciding what to wear. If this is a perennial problem for you, one way of shortcutting the process is to create small 'rules', such as wearing a red tie on Mondays, a blue one on Tuesdays and so forth.

Try it now

To take away the pain of wondering what to wear each day (and to allow you to plan ahead with ease), create some rules. For example, on Mondays you might choose to wear black and white only and on Tuesdays a suit.

Suddenly the decision is made for you and you can concentrate on other, far more important ones, such as what to pack for lunch! (This is the reason why underwear and socks with days of the week printed on them are popular – they take away the need to make a decision.)

Key idea: Many decisions are unconscious

Certain decisions can be automated, allowing us to concentrate on making other decisions that need more quality thinking time.

Building in some patterns of thought is a great time-saving device but you need to know that, if taken to extremes, they can become, at best, limiting and, at worst, tip us over the edge. I experienced this when I had a client who had designed her life on a tight schedule, with every evening covering a certain task or domestic duty to ensure that her job and home ran smoothly. One day she was invited to the wedding of a friend, but she could not work out how to fit this into her schedule. Her timescale was so tight that attending an extra event for a whole afternoon and evening meant moving other tasks or simply not doing them, which she was not prepared to do. Mentally, she found this situation to be similar to an unfathomable puzzle and it nearly resulted in her having a breakdown. Her unconscious schedule suddenly became a conscious act, and it dominated her thoughts. She literally became a slave to the process that was intended as her salvation.

> **Remember this: Try to be flexible**
> Organizing or automating parts of your life can cut down on the number of conscious decisions you have to worry about making – but build in flexibility to incorporate the fantastic surprises that life gives us.

We need a large proportion of our lives to be unconscious so that we can dedicate our brainpower towards solving more conscious decisions, the ones that really tax our thoughts. It is only when something goes fundamentally wrong with our unconscious decisions that they will float like bubbles to the surface of our consciousness, ready to be considered anew.

We therefore need a proportion of our decisions to be unconscious, because this provides us with the time to consider more of the one-off, trickier decisions with full consciousness.

Making connections

Our brains love to make connections, and they start doing this even before we are born. Connections help to shortcut difficult decision making by providing a template for certain decisions. When you are young, the connections are new and flimsy, but as behaviours are repeated throughout our lives, the connections become ingrained and we become almost 'programmed' to respond in certain ways. For example, if you happened to meet someone you already know and they ask, 'How are you?' you are likely to respond without thinking in your usual way, probably with something like 'Fine, thanks' – even if you are not.

Quickly note down how you would typically make the following decisions:

▶ selecting a new item of clothing
▶ buying a house
▶ whether to change your bank (and if so, how to select another bank)
▶ which restaurant to go to for a celebration meal
▶ choosing the name of your child
▶ whether to ask your boss for a pay rise.

It is highly likely that in doing the above exercise you will have resorted to previous methods you found useful, and that you would not use the same methods for all the examples. You may have used methods such as:

▶ relying on the ideas or suggestions of others
▶ gut instinct
▶ random selection
▶ whether something 'feels' right
▶ cost
▶ parental choice
▶ a friend's (or family member's) choice or opinion
▶ advertising and/or happenstance
▶ going with the majority
▶ being highly structural and factual (perhaps using a chart or grid)
▶ flipping a coin (or 'chance')
▶ gathering evidence for a report or presentation.

You may have used a combination of all these methods. However, you must feel that the way you currently make decisions is not working for you, or you would not be reading this book. Making decisions in a haphazard way is not usually the best method for solving problems, and neither is making decisions in the same way every time. For example, you may flip a coin to decide between two restaurants to eat in, but I would suggest that this is not the best way to choose a name for your child!

Our neural connections come from our background environment and have been reinforced over the years (which is why we find ourselves taking on mannerisms and sayings from our parents or grandparents – they are just so familiar to us). Some of these connections are helpful to decision making in that they produce instant unconscious responses. However, we must also realize that they can be limiting. When we respond automatically and without independent thought, we can be severely restricting our options. It is similar to taking always exactly the same route to work every day: it's great because you can do it without thinking but not so good for experiencing new things: scenes, architecture and people, for example.

....

Key idea: Habits can be changed

We can unconsciously be tied into patterns of thinking or habits of behaviour that sometimes need to be challenged.

....

Fact: most people sign up for an account at the same bank as their parents, and are not interested in changing to another bank, no matter what it may offer. Like it or not, we fall into patterns of behaviour and those links that our brains make are lodged very firmly. These patterns can be useful but they can also blind us to other options. This is why we must be aware of the limitations of always making decisions in the same way without considering other methods or trying other ideas. It is a case of speed of response versus innovation. We will be discussing both of these in greater detail in Chapters 3 and 5.

Try it now

Make a list of some of the aspects of your life where you have simply followed the patterns of others. Are you happy with those decisions? Are there any that you need to challenge?

The benefit of allowing enough time

Have you ever felt pressured to make a decision and wished that you had more time? There is no doubt that some decisions do benefit from deep thought, but real life dictates that we need to be able to act fast in some circumstances. Even some fairly major decisions (for example, buying a house at an auction) may need you to think clearly and quickly in a tense environment. In these situations, time is not always available. You can undertake research and fix a price band but, once the bidding starts, you have to think fast and clearly if you are to buy the property without exceeding your budget.

However, it is helpful to be able to consider a decision without being rushed, and in some instances it can be useful to buy yourself more time. This is not because you are slow at making decisions but because it gives you time to research the background, during which, more information may come to light. An informed decision is always better than a stab in the dark.

Remember this: Quick decisions can be good decisions

It is an interesting fact that decisions taken after a great deal of deliberation are not exponentially better than those made 'on the hoof'. Taking five times longer to make a decision does not mean that the outcome will be five times better. It pays to remind yourself of this when you are pressed into making a fast decision. A quality outcome is not guaranteed by the amount of time you have invested in making the decision.

Decision blockers

Even people you consider to be brilliant at making decisions will have times of indecision, times when they feel stymied and unable to think clearly. I am sure we all know how it feels suddenly to be unable to move forwards or select the best option, or even to experience full 'decision paralysis'. Unfortunately, life is not a game show and you cannot phone a friend or ask the audience. You feel the whole world closing in on you as you mentally struggle with the options being offered. This may happen for a number of reasons, some of the more common of which are:

▶ **Having too much invested in the situation** – sometimes the further you are from a situation the more objective you can be about it, and therefore the easier the decision becomes. If we fear personal loss, it makes the decision even more difficult.

▶ **Imposing a time limit** – it is no accident that on game shows the contestants have to respond to questions or make decisions with the clock ticking away. This is not just to keep the activities short for the programme schedule: it also puts people under pressure. The message that you have an important decision to make causes much more stress when someone adds, 'in the next three minutes'.

▶ **Too many options** – we will discuss options later in this book, but if there are too many choices, decision making becomes harder. It is no accident that salespeople in shopping stores try to narrow your choice to two or three items by using searching questioning techniques. It is much easier for you to decide on one item from two or three options than from 20. When the choice seems overwhelming, we walk out of the shop with nothing.

▶ **Failing to define the problem** – if you have ever been in a situation where another person jumps in on your conversation and offers advice with no prior knowledge of you or your subject, you will know how ridiculous and annoying this can be. You will probably think, 'No, you're wrong. How can you offer advice when you don't know anything about this, me, or my situation?' This is similar to failing to define the problem. If you do not define it correctly, you are dealing with what you perceive to be the issues rather than what actually are the issues, and that means you might miss the point completely.

▶ **When you know that the outcome will be unpopular** – in an ideal world there would be one 'good' option and one 'not so good' but this rarely happens outside fairy books. This type of decision, when there is not one easy solution – just two unpopular ones, is often seen in government. Unfortunately, both outcomes will be difficult and unpopular for the people, but which one is less so, and which one is in the country's best interests for the future?

▶ **Worrying about what people think** – the decisions we make say things about us. What happens when we have to make an unpopular decision within our own team or for someone who may have an impact on our career? How does having this type of audience cloud our decisions? Are we in danger of becoming 'people pleasers'?

▶ **Emotional fever** – you know you should not have it, you know you do not need it, you know you don't really have the money – but *you want it*! Need I say more? Sometimes our emotions take over and we make purely emotional decisions based on how we feel at that moment. Emotional attachment is not only about other people, but it can also be about objects such as houses and cars.

Remember this: Decision blockers may protect you

Blocks may be there to protect you. If you cannot make a clear decision, then consider whether you are, in fact, the right person to be making that decision at all.

The rollercoaster effect

Something else to be aware of is that decisions may have a rollercoaster effect. This means that the decision is not always an end in itself, but has implications for further or future decisions. For example, choosing a sofa (because you loved it in the shop) before moving into your house may mean that the colour, style and fabric of the sofa will now dictate the rest of the room's furnishings. In other words, your decision to buy that sofa has had a domino effect on other aspects of the room. This can make life easier, in that you have narrowed down the choice of other furnishings (having bought the sofa you now know you need to surround it with pale colours and light fabrics), or it could make life more difficult (where are you going to put the coffee table Mum gave you because it now does not look right with the sofa?).

This multiplication of one decision triggering more decisions is like stepping on to a rollercoaster that is going out of control. It's fine if we want to do this in our own lives but it does not look good in business, where you should have considered these factors before steaming ahead. In future chapters, I will show you how to analyse a problem so that this will not happen to you, but it's important to look out for it happening in other walks of life, too.

> **Key idea: All decisions have implications**
> All decisions have implications, which we need to explore.
> If we have to make an important decision, we need time to analyse it from several different perspectives to make sure that we are aware of as many of the implications as possible before we take the decision.

Working with your energy

Making decisions takes nimble brainpower. You can't operate effectively if you are feeling ill or sluggish. If you have a cold or feel under the weather, consider putting off any large decisions because you may just agree to something on the hoof that you live to regret. The point here is that colds don't last forever, so listen to your body. If your body is saying, 'I need all my energy internally,' then try to defer any big decisions until you can think more clearly.

If your lack of energy is due more to feeling down in the dumps or downtrodden in any way (rather than attributable to a virus), you will need to go on more of an offensive. You may need to:

▶ **Consider your diet** – are you eating healthily? Do you lack certain nutrients? Fish oil is known to be beneficial to brainpower as well as being good for joints. Think about what you eat and how to add additional nutrients to your food.

▶ **Take some light exercise** – there is a strong link between the brain and physical movement. You don't have to join a gym, but by moving regularly we really do exercise the brain. Think about it: if you suddenly forget something or lose your train of thought, you are more likely to remember it if you return to the place where you were standing or if you re-enact your movements. Similarly, if you are stuck and unable to come up with new ideas, staying in the same position will not help. Go and make a coffee, chat to someone by the printer, walk around the block or simply do something different. Just a simple change in your movement or in your environment forces the brain to think differently.

▶ **Chat to friends** – often interaction with other people will increase your energy levels. All of us are similar to small dynamos and we can give and take power from each other. Some people may drain you of energy but others appear to have energy in abundance and radiate it out to others. Those are the friends you need to be interacting with when you feel low. Their energy and enthusiasm for life will transmit to your radar and you will feel much more positive after spending time in their presence.

▶ **Consider your own outlook on life** – to be fair, not everyone is a born optimist. However, thinking negative thoughts is not helpful when you are making a decision. If you have already decided that there is no solution to a problem, there is little impetus to try and find a way out. Changing your way of thinking, even if it is forced, can open up new avenues and lead you to explore other solutions.

Energy is a driving force for decision making and therefore you need to take responsibility for your own energy levels. This may mean changing your routine or way of life or even analysing your own thinking, but the results will make this worthwhile.

Key idea: Work with your energy
Work with your energy and find ways of increasing its power, to enable you to make faster and better decisions.

Losing the guilt

One aspect of decision making that holds us back is the fear of making the wrong decision and the guilt that accompanies it. It is easy for me to say 'Lose the guilt', but it is not so easy to do.

The further you move upwards in your career, the more decisions you will have to make. Management positions are all about taking decisions and managing risk; in a sense, this is what managers are paid for. You therefore need to think about the types of decisions you (and your manager) need to make in the course of your work.

You cannot get away from making decisions all your life, that would be impossible, but if you really don't like making decisions and you find the outcome of each decision makes you feel sad, bad or miserable, look for a job that includes less decision-making responsibility. Since others will judge you on your decision-making ability, especially if you are in a senior position, it can put a significant amount of pressure on you when you already feel vulnerable.

One way round this – and that will lessen the impact of your feelings – is to ensure that you can fully justify every decision you make, and this is what we explore in Chapter 6. If you feel justified in your actions, you will be less concerned if someone criticizes the outcome. Ready to read on? Let's just consolidate the main points first.

▶ We need to know how we make decisions before we can tell whether we are using the most effective method for each type of decision.
▶ We make many decisions unconsciously because life would be too difficult if we had to make every decision consciously.
▶ You can streamline your life by making some decisions in advance, creating 'rules' – although you can take this too far.
▶ Not every decision has to be made immediately; there is a case for allowing some time to pass so that you can research additional background facts.
▶ Some issues can cloud our decisions, and in these instances it can be better to separate the decision itself from other factors surrounding it.

FOCUS POINTS

Chris works at Peters & Sons, a print works in Bidchester. He has recently been appointed supervisor and would like to move eventually into management, but Peters & Sons is a family-run company and has no management training in place. Chris has decided to take matters into his own hands and enrolled on a supervisors' programme at the local adult education centre. To supplement his studies he has decided to buy a few books to help him with key aspects of his career and course. He knows that decision making is important if he is to move forward in his job because a lot of his work entails making decisions and he knows that making a wrong decision can ruin a small company like Peters & Sons. From working through the self-assessment, Chris learns that he is not afraid of taking decisions but does not know any techniques and would really like some help.

Pat is a hairdresser. She has managed a salon called Up-do for the past seven years. The owners now want to sell and Pat has been approached to see whether she would like to buy the salon. She is tempted, but knows nothing about keeping books and making sure the salon runs at a profit. She knows that if she does not buy the salon it is likely to close. There is another buyer interested and they do not want it to remain as a hairdressing salon. Pat knows that the first thing she has to do is make that critical decision, but she has never been good at making decisions and so she decides to buy a book on the subject. After doing the first exercise, Pat realizes that she makes decisions in all sorts of ways in her life but that she may not be using the most effective technique for each problem.

Next Step

You should now have given some thought to your current style of decision making, and whether you tend to make decisions based on the ideas of others and are happy with their outcome. In the following chapter we will be looking at the key skills necessary for decision making, and how to develop and enhance your current skills.

2

Developing the right skills

Goal: To strengthen the skills needed for decision making, and to develop others.

Self-assessment

Read the following statements about decision-making skills, and say how much you agree with them by circling one of the numbers. If you disagree with the statement circle the 1, if you neither agree nor disagree circle the 3, and if you fully agree circle the 5:

I understand which skills enhance decision making	1	2	3	4	5
I revisit and review my skills every six months	1	2	3	4	5
I am always happy to attend training programmes	1	2	3	4	5
I observe the skills that others have and try to emulate them	1	2	3	4	5
I am confident that I have all the skills I need to make great decisions	1	2	3	4	5
I actively search for opportunities to enhance my skills	1	2	3	4	5
I always volunteer for challenging work that will stretch my potential	1	2	3	4	5
I have regular meetings with my manager or a mentor/colleague/friend to discuss my skills and abilities	1	2	3	4	5
I see myself as an ever-developing work in progress	1	2	3	4	5

I believe that all skills can be developed further	1 2 3 4 5
Now add up your score and put the total in the box. **Total score =**	

Score	Result
41–50	You are able to identify a wide range of the skills required for decision making and you can match your own skills against them. You regularly revisit your skills through meetings with your manager, a mentor or a friend, and are happy to develop yourself further when required. You not only attend training programmes but you also look for development opportunities around you.
26–40	You are fairly confident in your range of skills but perhaps you don't revisit them as much as you could. Do you have regular meetings with others to discuss your progress or suitable training opportunities? Do you believe that all skills can be developed further? Once you have read this chapter, return to this questionnaire and see whether you have changed your thinking.
Below 25	You may lack confidence or not have the support you need around you. All skills can be developed further but it helps to be able to target specific skill sets to help you with decision making. This chapter will help you think through these skills in a logical way. When you have read it, take an extra moment to reflect on how your views on development may have changed and grown.

Skills play a huge part in our lives. Every time we go through a situation we learn and grow from the experience, whether that be in a positive or negative way. We can choose to let these experiences pass us by without a second thought or we can choose to focus on them.

Imagine that you have just bought a new car. You know you negotiated well and you feel that you secured a reasonable deal. As you leave the showroom, do you:

▶ congratulate yourself on your good fortune and go home, all the time thinking only of when you can actually drive the car?
▶ reflect back on the negotiation, asking yourself: Were they any other strategies I could have used? What was the tipping point? Who was in control of the negotiation? What went right?

It is only by using the second approach that you are reflecting on your skills, how you used them, and whether you could improve in the future.

The decision-making process

When we make decisions we divide the process into sections, as follows:

1 Managing the initial situation
2 Analysing the situation
3 Fostering creative solutions
4 Sorting, ordering and evaluating possible solutions
5 Making a selection and creating a strategy
6 Planning how you will go forward
7 Bringing others on board
8 Taking action
9 Evaluating the outcome

First, let's look at the process in detail using an example of an everyday decision – later we will analyse these points further and look at the skills you need at every step. The scenario is that your partner has suddenly asked you to go out for a meal with them; the decision is yours as to where to go:

1 Managing the initial situation – you are shocked but pleased. It is exciting to be asked out and you may be quite emotional, and

therefore you may find your thoughts dashing all over the place. You may not be thinking calmly and rationally at this stage.

2 Analysing the situation – you may be asking yourself many questions, such as: Why are they doing this? Why tonight? Is it an anniversary you have forgotten? Are you celebrating something or is there a message in there?

3 Fostering creative solutions – now the fun bit, where to go. You don't have to decide just yet but you may be thinking of all kinds of restaurants, bars and clubs. Do you want something 'everyday', such as a pub meal, or some more exotic fare? Or perhaps you really do have something to celebrate and so you can justify a trip to that new high-class restaurant you have had your eye on?

4 Sorting, ordering and evaluating possible solutions – lots of ideas are now in the air but they all have implications. If you want to drink you cannot drive, and so if you want to drink alcohol the place has to be within walking distance, or you need a taxi. If you do not feel like dressing up, you will not want to set off for a restaurant where you may be refused entry for being too informal. Perhaps you remember one restaurant where you had particularly good service, or one that was very friendly. You will create your own criteria and search accordingly.

5 Making a selection and creating a strategy – now you will make your choice and run through (in your mind) how the evening will work out

6 Planning how you will go forward – you expand your thinking to how you will travel to the chosen venue, and what you will wear. Do you have to make a reservation? Do you need to order a taxi? Will you need a childminder? Do you have pets that need walking before you go? Do you have some work to do first, do you need to cancel anything else you had planned, or do you need to factor in some pampering time?

7 Bringing others on board – you need to present your idea to your partner. After all, they may have other factors in mind (such as price) of which you are unaware. You will need to be persuasive and able to convince them that your chosen venue is the right one.

8 Taking action – hooray, you actually have the meal in the venue you have chosen.

9 Evaluating the outcome – how did the evening go? Did you manage to select the right venue for the occasion? Did everything go according to plan?

Phew! You might be thinking, 'Organizing a venue for a meal out should never be so complicated!' – and often, in truth, it will not seem like this, but all the steps are there. However, going through the planning and thinking steps (1–7) before the actual meal may take minutes and happen in your head rather than be written down. In other words, we go through this process even if we are unaware of it.

Naturally, if you were making a heavyweight business decision, you might write every step down and take time over each one. For example, if you were deciding whether to go with a new supplier for your business needs, you may well spend quite some time in each section, and so let's look at the skills required at each step.

Remember this: The team can decide

Not every step has to be undertaken by the same person. If you feel that, for now, your skills are not so developed in fostering creative solutions, involve others. This can be great for team building and encouraging everyone to feel involved.

1 MANAGING THE INITIAL SITUATION

Sometimes the decision is yours, and at other times it is foisted on you. You may be willing or unwilling, aware of the situation or totally unaware. It could come as a complete surprise or a welcome conclusion. Whatever it is, it is likely to trigger an emotional reaction.

Try it now

Think back to the last time you had to make an important decision. How did you react? How did you feel? Write down your response on a piece of paper.

People who have to make an important decision may initially react in a variety of ways. They may be:

- ▶ shocked
- ▶ scared
- ▶ worried
- ▶ excited
- ▶ pleased
- ▶ angry.

These are just some of the emotions you may experience. This show of emotion may then translate into body language that is difficult to hide, such as pulling a face or throwing your arms into the air in disbelief. If your reactions are very overt and visible, they may alarm others or make you appear unable to cope (for example, it would be difficult to accept that everything is all right in the office if you could see someone in a room waving their arms around and looking hostile).

Being skilled in the awareness and control of our body language is not about hiding situations or being false, it is about being able to react in the most appropriate manner for the situation. This type of control is often called 'emotional intelligence' as we are able to control our impulses and select the correct responses in different situations.

Key idea: Emotional intelligence is needed
> The more aware of our body language we are, the easier it is to control. Therefore you need to become familiar with your own mannerisms and expressions so that you can control or change them if they are inappropriate to the situation.

Key skill(s) in this section: awareness of your reactions, controlling your reactions

To develop this skill you could: start immediately noticing how you react in different situations. Ask others how expressive you are, and how you demonstrate your feelings. Reflecting on recent decision-making situations, ask yourself how you initially reacted and whether that affected the outcome. Start to notice how you react in meetings and groups – can you control that reaction?

2 ANALYSING THE SITUATION

When you analyse a situation you need to delve deep in the hope of creating a better understanding of the issues. You can do this by asking yourself the 'Five Whys' made famous by Taiichi Ohno. The theory behind the Five Whys form of analysis is that each level digs deeper into your thoughts. For example:

▶ Why 1: why are they asking me to take on this project?
Answer: because I have the right skills for it.

▶ Why 2: why do I have the right skills?
Answer: because the organization has invested in me by letting me go on courses.

▶ Why 3: why am I asked to attend these training programmes?
Answer: to demonstrate how the organization invests in staff and to upskill all staff for situations like these.

▶ Why 4: why should the organization invest in staff to this extent?
Answer: because they believe in their staff and want them to succeed.

▶ Why 5: why do they want them to succeed?
Answer: because they want them to feel competent in their work and good about themselves.

However, you also need to see the problem from many different sides. Suppose you have been asked to take on a project. Who else could they have asked? Why this particular project? Why now? Could the project be split or shared (to reduce the additional workload)? Could someone else support or mentor you?

Analysis is thus both drilling down into the subject and also looking at it from other sides so that you gain a full appraisal of the problem or issue. If you watch detective programmes, you will be aware that in every situation there may be hidden factors, and this is the same in any decision-making situation. You may not always be able to be aware of every nuance, but try to find out what you can.

Key skill(s) in this section: to be able to analyse the situation and gain a full understanding of the background and any implications.

To develop this skill you could: try using the Five Whys technique above to enable you to explore a situation. Ask for the full background on any issue, *before* taking it on. Go and speak to other people; find out what they know.

3 FOSTERING CREATIVE SOLUTIONS

When we have to make a decision, it is quite usual for us to come up with one or two initial quick decisions. We think to ourselves, 'Well I could do A or B.' However, if we react to this (and sometimes we have to when the decision is urgent), we will be limiting ourselves to our first-level (surface) thoughts, the ones that come easiest to us. In other words, we have not tried to develop second-level solutions by playing about with possible ideas.

If solutions pop into your head easily, and you feel they are the right ones, then that is fine; make that decision now. But, if you had waited, you might have come up with a more creative solution, something that would have fitted your situation better. That might have opened up even more possibilities. Sometimes it is better to build in some thinking time, even if you are fairly sure you know your decision already.

I will cover many more creativity-inducing techniques in the next chapter, but for now we are concentrating on your skills and how you can develop them.

Key skill(s) in this section: finding creative solutions is about thinking differently and expanding on the number of ideas you may generate.

To develop this skill you could: try holding back from making snap decisions. Build in a bit of thinking time by telling people, 'I will be back with my decision a little later,' and then take yourself off into another environment, or ring a friend. Read through the following chapter and see where you can build increased rates of creativity into your thinking skills.

4 SORTING, ORDERING AND EVALUATING POSSIBLE SOLUTIONS

The problem with unleashing creative solutions is that it can be like opening a box full of pick-'n'-mix sweets – they spill out everywhere and there are just so many of them! What you need is a way of grouping them, putting them in some kind of meaningful order, so that you can manage them in some way.

One simple way of ordering your ideas is to write them all on separate cards. (Sometimes just the act of writing them on cards will stimulate more ideas or deeper thoughts about them.) Now put your cards into three piles:

1 This is definitely worth considering.
2 There is something in this – it interests me.
3 I don't think this one is going anywhere.

Immediately discard pile number three, setting it aside. Now we are left with ideas that are definitely worth considering and some that have promise but need developing further.

Ask yourself this question: how much time do I have to make this decision? If you do not have long, you are looking only at the first pile. However, if the decision can wait a little longer, push the first pile to one side and bring the second pile to the forefront.

Note on each card the words that interest you. Use coloured pens to highlight specific words and let your mind float again. What is needed to turn this second-pile idea into a first-pile idea? Who do I need to engage? Can anyone else help me with this?

Now be really strict and give yourself a time limit, so that the decision does not go on for ever. (It can be helpful here to use a food timer set to how much time you have allowed. This frees your mind from clock-watching and it can always be reset.) Commit to the decision in your diary: 'At 3 p.m. tomorrow I will have my five top decision outcomes and I will select the one that is the best fit.'

Key skill(s) in this section: you need to be able to organize and record information in a meaningful way in preparation for a selection.

To develop this skill you could: try working with someone else on a large decision; perhaps they cannot decide whether to move house or which car to buy. By helping someone else through this process, you will learn a lot for yourself. Invent another way of ordering the decisions, such as creating a grid or chart.

5 MAKING A SELECTION AND CREATING A STRATEGY

Now that you have your top ideas you need to make a final selection. The size of your decision will often dictate how detailed the selection should be. In some instances, there is one clear winner and therefore it is fairly obvious what the decision will be, but at other times it may not be quite so straightforward. Context can also be important. For example, if you were deciding which house to buy for your family, there may be little comeback, but if you were deciding where to invest your company's money, the shareholders may well want to know how you came to your decision, particularly if it all goes wrong.

Remember this: The selection must be credible and fair

If you are in a business situation, you are likely to be held to account for your final decision. How that decision was made then becomes very important, and therefore the selection must have credibility and be fair. When in business, I have found the following question to be helpful as a rule of thumb: How would this sound if read out in court? Would others believe how you came to that decision?

To make your final selection, it is helpful to have a number of criteria for judging your possible decisions alongside. For example, if you were trying to decide which house would suit your family best, you could have a grid with the houses along the top and the criteria (such as 'Must have three bedrooms') down the page. You can then mark each house against the criteria with a percentage of compliance. If the first house had three bedrooms you would put 100 per cent, but if the second had two bedrooms and a small office you might want to score it as 75 per cent because it has a third room, but you are not sure if it could be used as a bedroom until you check its dimensions, and so forth.

When you add up the percentages you should then have a clearer idea of the decision you should make, even if we just eliminate a few of the contenders. If you are able to make a full decision at this stage, you can then start planning a strategy for (in the house example) making an offer.

Key skill(s) in this section: organizing and being clear on criteria (if your criteria are too broad you will end up with too many options at the end, too narrow and you might end up with none).

To develop this skill you could: practise creating meaningful criteria to select against. Create a grid for a decision and complete it. Reflect on how it feels when you want one outcome to be the 'right' one but it does not score highly enough.

6 PLANNING HOW YOU WILL GO FORWARD

Depending on the context of your decision, once it is made you will need to have a plan in place to carry it forward and start implementing it. Often when we make a big decision – let's say to have an extension put on our house or even to start a family – we often do not think beyond making the decision, because at the time that seems mighty in itself. However, once the decision is made we need to start thinking ahead, to how it is going to be implemented.

This plan could be as simple as a short note in a diary or as long as a full project plan, with dates, milestones and deliverables. Of course, it may also include other people who will need to know how the decision was made, and the next steps for making the outcome a reality.

Key skill(s) in this section: forward thinking, organizational skills.

To develop this skill you could: try watching the news and take any decision made on that day – there is usually a political one – and see whether you can guess five key tasks that will make this decision a reality. Also consider a large task, such as having a conservatory built onto your property, and then chunking the work down into smaller tasks, such as: 1. Contact council to see if planning permission is required; 2. Contact three builders for quotations.

7 BRINGING OTHERS ON BOARD

There is no change without people. Organizing people to work with you, and in some cases for you, means that they must be engaged in what you are trying to achieve. Perhaps you need them to help you in some way, otherwise your chosen option will not work, or maybe you need them to trust you. Whichever is appropriate, you will need to win, if not their hearts and minds, initially their willingness to listen.

Key idea: Tailor your message

> When you want to engage with people, consider carefully the message you want to give and how you are going to give it. If you are giving your message to a large group, you may need to be more general, but if it is in a one-to-one context, listen to how the person uses language. If we give our message to people in a manner with which they are familiar, using the type of metaphor they use and perhaps phrasing our words as they do, they are more likely to take on board our message.

Taking others with us is not just about selling our decision; we also want them to engage in the ethos behind the decision. In other words, we don't want them to follow us blindly and do the change we ask. If we want everyone to be fully engaged, they need to know *why* the change is so important, and *what* we hope to deliver with it. This way, they will still undertake the decision, but with a different attitude and level of understanding.

Key skill(s) in this section: dealing with people, influencing people.

To develop this skill you could: try a spot of reading around the subject. Dealing with people can be tricky but there are a host of books available to help you. If you need to deal with people regularly, you may also like to attend a course on neuro-linguistic programming (NLP), which will give you many techniques for engaging people and groups.

8 TAKING ACTION

No decision is complete if it does not lead to action. (Even the decision to do nothing for now is still an action.)

Actions can vary from a web of major, multifarious actions that are required to implement a huge deal or decision, to small one-off actions. To make anything happen requires impetus.

Key skill(s) in this section: being decisive, driving forward.

To develop this skill you could: try to be consciously decisive. Tell yourself that you HAVE made the right decision and that it WILL work. You need to remain clear on your goals and not waver. All decisions need to go forwards, so prepare a plan of action that takes you step by step nearer to your decided outcome.

9 EVALUATING THE OUTCOME

All decisions will need evaluating at some point. How did it work out? Did it deliver what you wanted? If not, why not? What could have been done differently?

When evaluating, it is important to go back to the original matrix for the decision and look again at the criteria. You have to accept that, in some cases, the criteria change and that is not your fault. For example, you may have bought a lovely, neat flat based on your own needs but find that six months after moving in you are either expecting a child or an elderly relative needs to move in with you. This does not mean that buying the flat was a bad decision – you can only work with the information you have at the time. What it does mean is that you are ready for more decisions: Can we make this work? Do we need to move again?

Key skill(s) in this section: evaluating, planning for the future.

To develop this skill you could: try going back to your original decision and looking at the criteria. Was there any part of the analysis that could have indicated that this further change had been on the horizon? If the indications were there, how can you make sure you are more thorough next time?

▶ Considering the role of skills is hugely important in decision making. Skills can be lost if they are not used, but you can also develop and strengthen them by practising them regularly.

▶ The skills discussed in this chapter can be gained in a variety of ways and are very much a part of everyday life.

▶ If your decision includes other people, you will need to consider how you engage with everyone and use your influence wisely.

▶ Where your decision is unpopular, you may need to incorporate advanced 'people' skills using techniques such as NLP.

▶ Make sure you consider your skills every six months and also gain feedback from others.

FOCUS POINTS

Chris wants to move into management but he is aware that, as he has had no training, his skills may be sorely lacking. Peters & Sons is a company that has grown 'organically' and therefore does not have a large structure or any bespoke training. Chris has sought the advice of his tutor at Bidchester Adult Education Centre, where he is on a supervisors' programme, because he knows that decision making will form a large part of his day as a supervisor. She has shown him how to break the decision-making process into sections, and from those sections Chris can see where he feels confident and less confident. She assures him that 'decision making' will be part of the course, but if he does this small amount of preparatory work first, he will not only fly through that module but also, because this aspect is so important to Chris, pick up skills needed for other parts of the course. Chris is delighted because he knows that this skill could not only make his career but also grow the business.

Pat's first big decision is whether to buy the salon or not. If she does not buy it, the shop will probably be used for another function and the staff sacked, but she also knows that she cannot be sentimental about this. It is a life-changing decision and she is not sure where to start until she sees the nine-point steps to making a decision. Apart from the last point on evaluation, Pat decides to use this as a framework for going through the decision process of whether or not to buy the salon. She even goes as far as asking the other staff for their views and involving them in the process because she knows that if she does decide to go ahead, she will need their help. One member of staff even has the idea of each hairdresser earning 'points' for attracting new customers, which they can then save up for a bonus gift – an original idea that Pat had never thought of but the staff were keen to try. Pat has all her information and decides to go ahead and put a bid in for the salon. It is a brave decision but one that she now feels is well-thought-out.

Next Step

You should now have an appreciation of the skills you may need to develop to be great at making decisions. As in the case studies, you can use the nine-step plan both to check your skills needs and as a process for making a decision. Step 3 centred on creativity and generating more options, which will now be discussed further.

3

Generating more ideas and options

Goal: To expand the number of options open to you as decision maker.

Self-assessment

Read the following statements about creativity, and say how much you agree with them by circling one of the numbers. If you disagree with the statement circle the 1, if you neither agree nor disagree circle the 3, and if you fully agree circle the 5:

I always have plenty of options available to me	1 2 3 4 5
I feel very creative	1 2 3 4 5
I like playing games and puzzles	1 2 3 4 5
I often allow myself to daydream	1 2 3 4 5
I find my mind is constantly making connections	1 2 3 4 5
I always involve others when trying to figure out problems	1 2 3 4 5
I believe that everyone is creative	1 2 3 4 5
I feel positive about being given a conundrum to figure out	1 2 3 4 5
I believe there are techniques that can help me sort out problems	1 2 3 4 5
I believe that if you don't open up to more options you might miss an opportunity	1 2 3 4 5
Now add up your score and put the total in the box. **Total score =**	

Score	Result
41–50	You feel that you have a number of creative options open to you and you regularly tap into your creativity. You involve friends and the team in helping you and this can be useful for generating yet more ideas, and can also help to win them over to the final decision, because they feel that they have contributed. You start with a positive view – which is always helpful.
26–40	You feel fairly creative, perhaps more in some situations than in others. You may lack confidence in your own skills, or perhaps you were told off for daydreaming when you were young. You don't recognize that you have a wealth of creativity inside you just bursting to get out. You may miss a trick by not always involving others, but this may be because of your lack of confidence or concern about what other people will think.
Below 25	You may feel that you are not very creative, or perhaps in the past you have had a bad experience concerning creativity. I can assure you that everyone is able to expand their creativity if they truly want to. This chapter will explain why creativity is so important in decision making and show you a number of ways to increase your levels of creativity. Give it a go and stretch your mind into new spheres.

Why is creativity so important in decision making? The answer is that when you need to make a decision you need the largest pool of ideas possible, so that you select the most appropriate choice. How many times have you made a decision in a hurry because you initially thought that there were no more than two real options or solutions, only to find out later that there were other options, had you waited? Let's put this in a scenario. Imagine that you live in Kent and the company you have been working for since you left school is relocating to Scotland. You will probably think that initially you only have two choices:

▶ find a new job in Kent
▶ move to Scotland.

Just for a moment, imagine that you are that person. OK, you don't know the context (or where their family live, how many children they have and so forth), but just let your mind wander a little, and note down what other options might be open to this person.

When I did this exercise I came up with ideas such as:

▶ doing some of the work from home and flying up to Scotland twice a week
▶ requesting a change of job so that it could be done from home
▶ staying at a bed and breakfast (or small hotel) for part of the week
▶ relocating the family farther up the country – but not to Scotland – and commuting from there
▶ suggesting that, although the company is relocating, a small team remains in Kent to handle southern and European enquiries
▶ the whole family pitching in to buy a castle in Scotland and all relocating
▶ suggesting that they open an office in Calais (although still a commute, it would be nearer for you).

You will have found even more ideas. While many of these options may not be realistic, there could still be a germ of an idea in there, and having an increased number of options will make you feel more positive about the future and more in control. In situations such as these, many people fear having no choice because they feel cornered. Being able to offer some alternatives, even if they are rejected later, can place the individual back in control.

Remember this: There are many options
You need to open up to different options before focusing down on the final choice. This will not only give you more ideas but will also make you feel more in control of the situation.

How creative do you need to be?

So many people tell me, 'It's OK for you, but I am just not that creative.' Sound familiar? Well, let me smash that fallacy right now. We are all born as creative as we need to be – it is there, dormant in all of us and just needs awakening.

Where many of us get a little stuck is that we either think that creativity should be:

▶ limitless – in other words, that creative people can come up with an endless supply of alternatives. Every barrel has a base and for each person to come up with just one or two additional ideas is good, so stop being too hard on yourself.
▶ sensible or useful – that every creative idea should be instantly useable. The truth is that some of the most unusable and whacky suggestions often act as triggers to other ideas that have potential merit, so go wild (especially when no one is looking).

Key idea: Even absurd ideas can get results
Drop the idea now that you must come up with a good selection of sensible options or lose credibility. Creative people are not afraid of suggesting the absurd, especially if it gets them one step nearer to a solution.

To stimulate your creativity, read the section on the subject (step 3) in the previous chapter and drop into your local art gallery for a little mental exploration. Ask yourself some bizarre questions, such as who said that someone's face could not be painted in blue and neon yellow (like an Andy Warhol print)? Is it OK to have a photograph with the subject not in the centre? Artists constantly stretch the boundaries without apologizing for it. Try stretching the boundaries of your creativity with some of the exercises in this chapter.

No man is an island

When you did the previous exercise you were probably on your own, and you probably did not ask anyone to help you. This is very worthy but, if you want a variety of ideas, you may find that you are limited by your own experience.

We are all limited to what we know and have experienced. In other words, our brain can only work with what it has already seen or experienced. For example, if I told you that I had been on a safari and seen a lemonitis, you would not know what I was talking about, unless you had seen a picture somewhere or read about the creature. You would not know whether it was as tall as a giraffe or whether it was an insect because you are attempting to pull together information in your brain from the library of life you have already lived. By the very nature of your brain, this is limited to one person – you. However, add another person to the conversation and they will have had different experiences and so the pool of thinking becomes greater. Interestingly, the number of ideas you will have will more than double because there would be your ideas, their ideas, and the ideas created from the talking, discussing and interaction between you both that you would never have come up with alone. Add more people to the mix and you have a massively increased, fertile pool of knowledge and experiences; in fact, the more diverse people are, the richer the creativity and ideas will be.

Therefore you should be actively seeking diverse people to help you bounce ideas around and make creative connections that will aid your decision making. If you have a team at work, involve them. If you don't have a team, use family members, mentors, colleagues or create a 'crazy thinking group' to help everyone start thinking outside the box. If you have the opportunity to develop an 'action learning set' or be involved in one, this is a great opportunity for creative thinking. Members of an action learning set usually come from different backgrounds, areas of work or disciplines and they work on solving problems. The key to helping the 'problem owner' lies in their lack of knowledge, as they then have no preconceptions and it is up to the problem owner to put their suggestions in context. Action learning sets have spawned many a great solution or decision to a dilemma, as it is sometimes through the innocent question that we find insight.

(NB: Before you search the Internet, there is no such thing as a lemonitis – I just used this word for illustration.)

Unrelated objects

Here is a fun one to get you started. Your brain loves games and it likes to play. It likes to be challenged by odd objects into making strange connections. Here is the decision: you don't know whether to change your car this year for a new one. Your car is not old and decrepit but you would be changing it in the next couple of years anyway, and there is an offer on at the local dealership that is tempting. You are not sure what to do.

How did you do? Examples using the three objects mentioned above may be:

▶ pen – am I 'writing' the car off? Should I be thinking of the car as more disposable (like a pen)?
▶ banana – is there any way to bend the rules? Perhaps I need to 'peel' back the deal at the garage and see the true costs that may be hidden inside.
▶ can of drink – how handy and portable would the new car be? Do I need to think about how my other car would be disposed of (recycling)? Do I simply need refreshing?

Get the idea? You are not looking for an outright solution because we are not closing down yet; we are still at the 'opening all possibilities' stage. We want to make sure that we ask all the right questions about the problem because that alone will guide us towards a decision.

Inspired by an apple falling, Isaac Newton went on to discover gravity. It is said that Archimedes discovered the displacement of water theory while stepping into a bath. Unrelated objects or actions often trigger great ideas.

Doodle doo

Are you a secret doodle-meister? If so, this could be the secret to unlocking your creativity. We take in information in different ways and our brains store pictures differently from words. We can look at a picture and find that it provokes an emotional reaction in us. What this means is that we are not just seeing the image but 'experiencing' it in some way. Images can make us laugh or cry, or move us to other reactions, and they can challenge our thinking and our values. Pictures can be powerful.

How can this help you stretch your creativity? Matching words and pictures results in stimulating different parts of the brain and therefore you are using more of the brain than words alone. Also, if you are more of a visual person, you will find it more comfortable to make connections with images than words. Many visual people find that they gather a great many ideas from watching a film and allowing their mind to freefall with the images from the film acting as stimuli.

Try it now

Make your own visualization box. Keep a stash of picture postcards in a drawer and, whenever you need to stimulate your creativity, select one at random and see what it is telling you. If you find this useful, make your own cards by cutting out pictures of furniture, kitchen items, artworks, people, buildings, scenes and abstract designs so that you can use them over and over again.

If you are an adept doodler, just presenting your decision dilemma pictorially can help you to think through the problem using that other part of your brain concerned mainly with images.

Music maestro

Another modality that stimulates creativity is our auditory function. Music has been proven to stimulate and affect us in an emotional way, but some people seem more receptive to music than images. Do you like music on while you are working or do you like silence? Do you find music helpful or do you find it hard to concentrate while it is playing? Perhaps, for you, the lyrics get in the way of clear thought or maybe they help you make more connections as in the unrelated objects above?

Mozart's music mimics a heartbeat and is widely reported to be ideal for stimulating the brain while studying. Perhaps a little Mozart can also help you to think more creatively. Alternatively, perhaps another composer such as Holst, who conveyed the planets so brilliantly, could take you to another world.

Some music will soothe you and allow you to drift off into your own world but you also need to think about what type of music stimulates and excites you. Everyone will have their particular preferences.

Key idea: Listen to music
Creativity needs energy to drive it forward, and energy can be stimulated through hearing your favourite music. Sort through your music collection and select at least one track that allows your imagination to run wild and another that stimulates you and gives you energy.

Kinaesthetic challenge

Some people are more adept than others at sensing or feeling a mood or atmosphere. They feel vibrations in the same way as other people hear music or see words or images. It is the same as when you attend a live concert and you actually feel the noise as the musical notes resonate in your body. This sensation creates a fuller experience and can stimulate your creativity in a more physical way. Similarly, some people are more sensitive to touch than others. They may find comfort in stroking a soft fabric or need to be in a certain environment where they 'feel' relaxed or stimulated.

Do you remember the squashy and tactile toys that once populated everyone's desk and were intended to reduce stress? The idea was that you squeezed them if you wanted to rid your body of stress, and they then magically reshaped themselves in readiness for the next assault. Those with kinaesthetic strengths as their main modality would find them not only stress-reducing but also a textural experience that could be stimulating.

Remember this: Use different modalities

We use all the modalities we have every day, but we tend to prefer some more than others. We each have an individual preference for one modality and that is the one we defer to most often. To become more creative, however, we need to tap into our less favoured modalities so that we appreciate and experience thoughts and sensations that would normally pass us by. Sometimes we have to force ourselves into using these other modalities, but the effects can be stunning.

Brainstorming

Brainstorming works best as a team activity. Of course, you can do it on your own but you will only reap your own thoughts, and that, as we have already discussed, will only provide a limited number of ideas.

Let's work with an example. Say you were clearing out a storage unit and you found that it was full of hard plastic VHS cases used for videos (which have now mostly been superseded by DVDs and newer technology). You have a decision to make with three immediate options:

- ▶ keep them (not really a great idea because you wanted the space for your own storage)
- ▶ dispose of them (you could do this but it is not really good for the environment and you might even have to pay to dispose of a large number)
- ▶ remarket them (Now you are talking! You could sell them as something else. The containers will be recycled and you will also make money – a double win!)

The question now is how are you going to do this? Brainstorming could be the answer. By gathering a few colleagues around you, you can use brainstorming to come up with a range of ideas for the cases. So how do we do that?

The reason brainstorming works best with groups is that several people together generate their own energy, and some of the best ideas come when everyone is firing off the ideas of others. All you need is a flip chart or large piece of paper and pens to display the ideas, so that everyone can see them. To start with, explain the rules:

1 Everyone is to totally freewheel with their thoughts. Nothing is too ridiculous or outlandish.
2 Everyone is to suspend judgement. It does not matter what other people think of any of the ideas; just carry on inputting and critical evaluation will come later.
3 Everyone is to contribute, add, combine, and improve any of the ideas as they wish.
4 There is no time limit.

Introduce the problem or decision to be made and then start the discussion, noting down the outpourings from the group. Once the initial ideas are out, there may be a small lull, but this does not mean that everyone is finished. Stay with it and the energy will rise again and further ideas will come, some of them deeper and more thought-provoking than before.

Here are the ideas that came from a group brainstorming about uses for VHS cases:

- building blocks for children
- jewellery cases
- boxes to keep loose change in
- small sewing boxes
- stick together to build a children's playhouse
- cemented together as a windbreak
- gift boxes
- boxes for holding fishing flies
- to make children's play stilts
- containers for toy soldiers
- sandwich boxes
- picture frames.

The next step is to decide which of the ideas has potential merit. In this example you may need first to delete the absurd ones, and then look at the costs, practicality and feasibility of the other ideas. You can do this in the group, but some individuals may become protective of their own ideas, which may cloud the decision making somewhat.

Don't forget to thank your group and tell them that you will let them know your final decision. Groups can often become so engaged in a brainstorming activity that they do not want to let go of the issue. Don't be surprised if you receive more suggestions in the days following the event, as the ideas keep coming.

Key idea: Brainstorming works

The reason brainstorming works is not just because of the numbers of people you use but also because the group is encouraged to lose its narrow vision and become less fixated on what the item for discussion was, leaving everyone to come up with a whole new set of ideas.

Adopt a questioning approach

Children are curious about the world and ask questions incessantly when they are young. At some point in our development, however, we ask fewer questions and eventually stop asking them altogether as we start to create our own ideas. This can limit us, because as soon as we stop asking others for their opinion or seeking an alternative view, we start to live only according to our own rules and knowledge base. This can be bad news for stimulating creativity.

Earlier in this book I mentioned the Five Whys approach. Asking why is not simply a technique: it should become part of the culture of your team if you want people to think more creatively

Consider this one question in relation to your decision: What would you do if money were no object and there were no boundaries? Your reply may surprise you. Encourage your team to ask questions and to challenge one another regularly. It will develop the team and expand their thinking.

Sleep on it

At some point we have all been encouraged to find a solution to a problem by 'sleeping on it'. This may sound odd (indeed, it is a cliché) but there is sound thinking behind the idea.

When we sleep our brain goes into freefall. It makes all the silliest and most foolish connections in its attempt to order our thinking. This is why dreams can be so bizarre. The brain is attempting to express the emotions and experiences of the day in a host of different ways. In contrast to when you are awake, when you have your sensors and filters refining your thoughts before they reach your consciousness, when you are asleep there is no censuring and your mind is free to wander through the full range of your unconscious. This unconscious mental freefall is wonderful for finding new and inventive solutions to problems, no matter how strange they may appear at first.

It is no accident that many highly creative people remember being told off at school for daydreaming. Daydreaming is like a wakeful sleep, allowing your mind the same level of freedom. Similarly, meditation can boost creative thinking because your conscious mind is focusing on one thing (such as your breathing or a repetitive word), while your unconscious mind is able to relax fully and playfully explore making other connections.

Try it for yourself. Next time you have a significant decision to make, think about the situation in detail as the very last thing you muse over before falling asleep. You may be surprised to discover that when you wake up you have the answer.

Remember this: Record your ideas

Make sure you always keep a notebook and pen by your bed, so that you can write down your thoughts and ideas as they come to you from your dreams.

Narrow your options

You now have several more options than before. However, you have yet to make the final decision. This is where we now need to drill down and choose one option. If you followed through the process in the previous chapter, you will be aware of creating criteria. Either use the three-pile technique covered in Chapter 2 or return to the initial problem and create some tight criteria by which you can begin to make your selection of possible decisions.

Remember this: Criteria should be relevant

If your criteria are too generous, you will find that too many options fall into a category and you are back to square one with the same list. Keep your criteria tight and relevant: for example, if you were deciding on a gift, 'inexpensive' is not tight enough and is a bit ambiguous. Try 'under £10' or 'between £10 and £15' – whatever is most relevant. The tighter your criteria, the easier the final decision will be.

- Creativity helps us open up our thought processes around a decision. It may not help us solve the problem on its own, but it will help us develop our thinking further so that more options are available to us.
- Creativity is in everyone and everyone can be creative.
- Work with all your modalities to create other experiences of the same event.
- Creatively opening up on ideas is only helpful if it aids your decision. Don't mistake it for procrastination – at some point you must make the decision.
- Create some really tight criteria against which to measure your options.

Although Chris is able to be creative in his work and oversees the graphic designers, he has not thought about being creative in a business context. His workers are a fairly macho bunch and he is not sure how they will interpret his desire to bring creativity into everyday work until the perfect opportunity arises. The print rooms need to expand but there is no more room in the surrounding buildings. To relocate the entire company would be unworkable and the cost prohibitive. Chris has been given this conundrum to solve as his first management task. He decides to invite everybody to a brainstorming session. By listening to his staff he finds out that one of the other units nearby will become available in six months' time. This means that their problem is only temporary. After brainstorming with the team they decide that they can manage for the next six months by taking over the two offices currently used by the finance staff, who could work flexibly from home. This will be possible until the other unit becomes available. Everyone is in agreement and the plan can go ahead.

Pat has decided to take on the salon but now she has to think about how she will afford it. If she uses her savings, she will have just enough to finance the purchase but not enough to pay salaries for the first few months, so if takings go down there will be a problem. If she takes out a loan to pay for the salon, the terms might be steep, and if the salon does not take off, what will she do? She could lose the salon and still be tied into the loan. Pat decides to be honest with the staff and tell them about her decision. She is astounded when the staff advise her to buy the salon outright (because this will make them feel safe) and tell her that they will each take only 75 per cent of their pay for the first two weeks to try and help get the new business off the ground. Pat thought she was on her own but in fact she learns that the team are right behind her.

Next Step

You have seen that trying creative techniques will help expand your options, and that setting tight criteria will enable you to make better decisions, based on the facts. However, in any decision-making situation we have to consider that something may go wrong. This is not being negative but about managing risk, and that is what we will discuss next.

4

Managing risk

Goal: To identify risk and minimize its impact on your decision.

Self-assessment

Read the following statements about managing risk, and say how much you agree with them by circling one of the numbers. If you disagree with the statement circle the 1, if you neither agree nor disagree circle the 3, and if you fully agree circle the 5:

I understand that every decision carries some form of risk	1 2 3 4 5
I feel comfortable identifying the risks attached to any decision I make	1 2 3 4 5
I can confidently rate and calculate risks	1 2 3 4 5
I understand the difference between managed and unmanaged risk	1 2 3 4 5
I am clear that the measurement of risk alone can become the criteria for the decision	1 2 3 4 5
I feel confident in engaging others in conversations around risk management	1 2 3 4 5
I believe that some risks have to be designed into the problem	1 2 3 4 5
I am aware of how risk can affect profit	1 2 3 4 5
I calculate and maintain a risk budget	1 2 3 4 5
I feel able to take decisions based on the level of risk I am calculating	1 2 3 4 5

Now add up your score and put the total in the box. **Total score =**

Score	Result
41–50	You feel able and confident to manage risk. You appreciate that every aspect of life includes risk to some extent and you build risk management into your decision-making process. You are also able to discuss risk openly and are not afraid to plan for things that you hope will not happen but often do. Even so, this chapter describes aspects of risk management of which you may be unaware and that may you may find useful.
26–40	You are fairly confident in your identification and management of risk. You understand and appreciate how the calculation of risk can help you make decisions but you do not always do this and may not be able to see how this can help you with all your decisions – not just business decisions. Read through the chapter and skim over the sections that cover familiar ground, concentrating more on areas or concepts new to you.
Below 25	This is an area where you may lack confidence or simply not be using all the tools and techniques to your advantage. You may not have considered risk as an intrinsic part of the decision-making process. This chapter will show you not only how to manage risk but also how risk can become the criterion that makes the decision, and you will also learn some great techniques for risk management.

Risk is all round us. Nearly everything we do incurs some form of risk. Even in the writing of this book there is a risk that:

▶ I may not complete it in line with my deadline
▶ I may not engage my reader (my writing style)
▶ I may have designed the book in a way that was not helpful to the reader (the format and contents)

…to name but a few.

My publisher is also taking a number of risks:

- ▶ Will I deliver on time and within schedule, to enable editing and printing slots and a marketing campaign to be booked?
- ▶ Is this a subject that you, the reading public, will be interested in?
- ▶ Will this book sell in sufficient quantities to make it a staple of the bookshelf?

…and so forth. They will not know whether their fears were justified or not until well after the book is published, but this does not mean that they should not consider these risks and take suitable action towards reducing them.

Thus, it is rarely possible to make decisions risk free, and there is no point in trying. However, we can do much to manage the risk and reduce the impact it may have on our decision. In the same way that you used creativity in the previous chapter to increase the number of options available to you, you are now going to learn how to measure risk in order to help manage those options and possibly make the final decision.

What is risk?

Managing risk is like taking out insurance. We are insuring for something that we hope will never happen but that could cost us dear if it does. When we arrange for property insurance we hope that we will never have to claim, but if we ever were the victim of fire or subsidence and had no insurance, we would be left not only homeless but, in all likelihood, owing money if we have not paid off the loan for furniture or our mortgage. Since we would never be able to pay to have our house rebuilt, we insure our property just in case (and in some cases, such as with mortgage lenders, there is no leeway – you *have* to be insured otherwise you are breaking the terms of your contract).

It is the same with risk. By highlighting that risk and creating a plan of management, you hope to be ready and protected if something happens.

> **Remember this: Risk can be calculated**
> Risk can be defined as:
>
> likelihood of something happening X the consequence

In the example above, the likelihood of you losing your home (obviously depending on where it is) could be classed as fairly low; after all, it does not happen every day and to most people never in their lifetime. However, the consequence of losing your home is high: it is very expensive to rebuild and re-equip a home. These are the calculations the insurance company will consider when setting your insurance premium (periodic payment). This is why it costs more to insure a property against flooding when you live in a floodplain area: the insurance company has to manage the risk and make adequate provision for payouts.

Why is calculating risk important?

Why are we so surprised that everything stops when it snows? It may not snow every year, but winter comes every year and brings with it temperatures low enough to cause snow, and so snowfall is fairly likely. Would it not be better to anticipate that it *will* snow and put some resources aside? After all, if it does not snow, we can keep the money in reserve or add it to our profits for that year.

You may be wondering what this has to do with decision making. If you were working for a council or the organization that supplies salt and snow ploughs to the highway authorities, anticipating snowfall would be crucial to your decision of how much salt and/or vehicles to buy in any one winter, and therefore how you manage your budget. You cannot say, 'Well, I don't know whether it will snow, so I will just go with whatever happens, when it happens,' because businesses and the public still need to be able to deliver their goods and travel to work, and services need to be able to continue as usual.

Storing salt and vehicles is expensive and takes up valuable space that could be used for other things. Buying in small amounts may not be enough in the event of a bad winter, and running out of supplies on day one will attract poor press coverage. Vehicles could be leased. This might cost more initially but there would be no storage or maintenance costs, so you would need to balance these factors. If you left your decision to the last minute and there is a snowfall lasting many days, you may not be able to find a snow plough to rent because of demand, and the price will have increased substantially. All these are decisions that someone in that job role needs to consider when running a winter service for the highways. They will also look at the probability of snow causing disruption. Any pattern that concerns the weather is probably not to be trusted completely but there may be trends – for example, a few years of milder winters – and they may decide to take a gamble on this trend.

When finally evaluating whether the resources were sufficient for the task, the manager can then look at whether they made the right decisions through the process. If there is salt left over, there may be ongoing storage costs, but if the salt was bought in the summer (when the price is lower) and the quantity is correct, there may be money left in the contingency budget, and the organization would consider this as profit that can be routed back into the business.

Remember this: Risk assessment is vital

Thinking about risk is not about being negative. Carrying out a risk assessment will help you ensure that resources are used more effectively, improve how you run your business and, in the long run, even save money.

What do we need to consider?

We need to take a full and complete picture of the situation so that we can consider the risks from every angle.

Measuring risk is not just about the financial elements of any decision. We also need to consider other risks such as the decision being late (time), people not being present to do certain tasks (available resources), and all the dependency issues. For example, most decisions have an impact on other decisions, such as when buying one particular house means that you have a different journey to work from the one you would have had if you had bought the other house you were considering. With one house you need a car, whereas with the other you can rely solely on public transport because there is a bus stop right outside. Suddenly you need to make decisions about how you will travel. Will you sell the car you currently have? Should you buy a newer car? Or is the car good enough for the regular journeys? Do you need to explore the cost of a bus permit?

To help us consider every aspect, it can be helpful to divide our decision into different sections, as shown below. Some of the areas overlap because, for example, there may be company policies that cover both the safety and security aspects of the decision.

To illustrate all these areas, take the example of having a new kitchen installed. You are in the process of selecting a company to fit your new kitchen. You have narrowed the choice down to three suppliers and you just need to make the final selection. All the prices fall within £50 of each other and there seems to be no clear cheap or expensive option. You decide to look at risk as a way of helping you to make your decision.

Key idea: Consider the risk
Look at risk as a way of aiding your decision.

Project-focused risk

When we think of project-focused risk, we must consider the types of risk that are directly related to the outcome of the decision. For the kitchen project, they include the following:

46

- ▶ Quality of the finish – have you seen their work somewhere else? What can be put in place to ensure that the quality of your kitchen will be as high?
- ▶ Quality of materials – are they brand names and is there a guarantee?
- ▶ Timescale – what is the risk if they don't meet your requirements? (You might choose the cheapest option but then have to spend money on eating out because they have not completed on time.)
- ▶ Finance options offered – what is the risk here? How much is the APR? Can you pay 50 per cent in cash? What if you lose your job and cannot make the repayments?
- ▶ People – do they have enough people to do a good job? What happens if the main worker is off sick?
- ▶ Penalties – what are the penalties if they abandon the job halfway through?
- ▶ Working hours – does the installation period straddle public holidays? Will they work weekends?
- ▶ Unforeseen problems – what happens if, during their work, they uncover other problems (such as a gas leak)?
- ▶ Changing my mind – can I change my mind about something halfway through installation? How definite do I need to be and what is the point of no return?

I am sure you can think of more risk factors that you may wish to consider.

Key idea: Measure the risk

Measure risk against your desired outcome.

Security-focused risk

We may not always immediately think of security in relation to risks to be considered with regard to a fitted kitchen, but here we are looking at such areas as the following:

- ▶ Are the workers insured to work on your premises? What happens if they have an accident, or if there is a gas leak or flooding?
- ▶ What happens to the data that you have entrusted them with, such as the details that you entered on the finance agreement? Will they sell that data on?
- ▶ Who is liable if the materials are stolen or stored incorrectly outside your house?

- Who is liable if their tools are stolen from your house?
- What is the situation if any other items are stolen from your house during the fitting?
- How is your insurance affected if the fitters leave the house unsecured while they fetch more materials?

> **Key idea: A breach in security could be expensive**
>
> A breach in security could cost you a great deal of money in the long run. If your personal details are sold on to other marketing companies, you may be plagued for years with calls and direct mail that you do not want.

Safety-focused risk

Safety needs to be considered not just in relation to the finished kitchen but also to how the workers are operating. If one of the workers falls from a ladder and sues the kitchen fitter, he will probably (financially) go under, and your kitchen may never be finished.

- What checks does the company have to protect its workers' safety? Are there relevant policies? Is protective clothing required?
- Does the company adhere to a health and safety policy for their staff?
- Are there guarantees for their work?
- Do they have the right legal qualifications to carry out and guarantee their work?
- What are they going to do to ensure *your* safety while the kitchen is being fitted? Will there be trailing wires? Will you be left without electricity? Will there be uneven surfaces that might trip you up?

> **Key idea: Unsafe could mean expensive**
>
> Considering risk around safety is essential because poor safety could lead to litigation problems and, in an extreme case, a house fire.

When you research the risks, you may find that one company demonstrates that it has considered all risks and has procedures to manage them in an effective way. If so, that is probably the one to choose, even if they are the most expensive. With something as complex as a fitted kitchen, you don't want to be dealing with hitches.

Naturally, once you have all the data to hand, you may still say that your overriding criterion is price. If this is the case, you have not lost anything by going through this exercise (if anything, you will have gained a lot of additional knowledge about each of the companies), but then you will revert to the cheapest option.

Contingencies

One of the reasons that people shy away from managing risk is that they don't even want to think about the cost of a large mistake. However, the truth is that if a decision is costed correctly and the budget managed regularly, there should be no nasty surprises.

To ensure that decisions do not suffer from a lack of funding, should things go awry, you will need to allocate part of your budget to a contingency fund. This money is not then wrapped in mothballs but visited regularly to see whether it is needed, and if not it becomes additional profit.

Contingency funding can be any amount, from the whole cost of replacement to a notional 10 per cent. It is for you to estimate, using your experience. Let's illustrate that in an everyday situation. You are going on holiday and you need to change some money into another currency to take with you as spending money. You know that most of your spending will be on credit card, so you decide to take £400 in cash. You could think that there is a risk that:

▶ you might lose the money or have it stolen, so you had better make sure that you have another £400 in your bank account, just in case
▶ you might lose the money or have it stolen, but it is a low risk (you have never lost money before), so you will keep an extra 10 per cent in your bank account available, just in case.

Both of these are contingency plans, but it is unlikely that you would keep another £400 in your bank account because it would be tying up too much of your capital. The risk of losing your money on holiday can also be managed to some extent (you could use a safety deposit box or draw out additional cash on your credit card, for example). It is more likely that you would use the second option and take a little extra, hidden, just in case – in other words, this will be your contingency fund. When you return from your holiday, if you have not spent the contingency fund it can be cashed in and you have a little bonus, money you had not considered. You can enjoy it after your holiday, perhaps going out for a meal or using the money as a down payment on the next holiday.

> **Remember this: Contigencies are your cushion**
> Having contingency money is a way of managing risk and is there to be used if you need it, but if it is not needed you can release it back into your budget to be diverted towards something else, as additional profit, or used to cushion your next decision.

Think back to the example of the kitchen being installed. You have looked at all the risks and decided that, after analysis, the company you have chosen to do the job is very professional and the overall risk that they may not finish the job is low (and you can partly manage this by not paying for the full job at the beginning, holding back your final payment until the kitchen is completed). However, there is a moderate risk that they will not complete the task in the allotted timeframe. If this happens, you may be without a kitchen for another few days, possibly even another week. If you don't have access to the kitchen, your costs will increase because you may have to:

▶ eat somewhere else, such as in a restaurant
▶ pay for your clothes to be laundered.

You decide that, rather than be caught out, you will put money aside for this. You estimate a possibility of five days of having to buy meals out (£20 per day) and two trips to the launderette (£20 each) and so you put aside £140. This is your contingency fund in case this situation arises. It makes you feel safe because suddenly the worry is taken away from you, the money is there should you need it, and you don't have to wait until the end of the installation to see whether you have enough. If after the first week you decide that everything is running to plan (or even ahead of itself), you can decide to remove some (or all) of the contingency money back into your funds. This is good money management, and you can congratulate yourself for managing the risks effectively.

> **Key idea: Keep the contingency fund fixed**
> Be firm with contingency cash; there is the contingency fund and then no more.

Using the traffic light system

So far we have looked at risk from the perspective of:

▶ considering risk as an important aspect of decision making
▶ identifying the risks surrounding a decision
▶ ensuring that you have resources put aside in a contingency fund to manage any risk that may occur.

However, I have only hinted at the fact that probability needs to be considered, too. In the kitchen example, I mentioned the risk of the installation team not completing the task, in which case you would need to pay for it to be completed by another company. I classified this as low risk, and it is one that could be managed by staging the payments. You would not need to set aside a sum of money in your contingency budget for that particular risk. We could think of many additional problems and extreme situations – such as the new kitchen blowing up or falling apart the minute the installation team have left – but these are also very low probability and therefore highly unlikely to happen.

Spend just a moment thinking through all the unlikely (but just possible) things that could go wrong when having a new kitchen installed, and then put beside each a probability ranking of whether you think that would actually happen.

I think you would agree that there is more probability of the workers not turning up than anything truly dramatic happening. For this reason, we need to consider the probability of each risk. One handy way of doing this is to use the traffic light system used in many large companies. This system is used to measure the *likelihood* of the risk – in other words, the probability of it happening.

Do not think automatically that the traffic light system is just a business system; it can work well in any situation, and can help you to identify the level of risk and make clear and fast decisions. In essence, the system uses the colours of traffic lights to indicate the level of probability of a certain risk:

▶ **Red** – this represents a major potential problem with a high likelihood of it happening. The consequences would be grave and could be dangerous. You either need to put in a large contingency plan to deal with this or even consider that the decision should not go ahead.

▶ **Amber** – the risk is moderate and likely to happen, but it can be managed. You need to ensure that you have clear contingency funding and monitor the situation regularly.

▶ **Green** – this risk is less likely and therefore can be managed through your contingency plan.

In our example, if the whole kitchen were destroyed by fire and had to be replaced, this would incur a high cost, but it is in the Green category because there is a low likelihood of it actually happening. However, the risk of some of the workers not turning up would be in the Amber category because it is a moderate risk but not sufficient to call a halt or reconsider the installation.

Making your decision based on risk

Risks are a part of everyday life, and you will find that when you start assessing them alongside your decision making, you will become much more adept at calculating them. You can also make your decision based on risk analysis.

If, after analysing the risks that accompany the decision, you consider the decision has too many Red traffic light risks, you may decide to say no. I am reminded of a very expensive decision a friend of mine once took. She bought a house at auction with the romantic notion of restoring it to its former glory. She told us hilarious stories about the ensuing disasters such as when, in the middle of eating Sunday lunch in the dining room, a whole wall fell down. Of course, it sounded funny later and made a great after-dinner anecdote, but at the time it was very upsetting. She has admitted to me on many occasions that had she undertaken a risk analysis or at least thought the situation through before buying, she would never have bid for the house. It has been a complete financial drain and emotional nightmare (more on emotional decision making in Chapter 8).

Whether you walk away from the situation or decide to go through with it, if that decision is based on risk analysis, you will know all the facts upfront and you will be less fazed (and possibly even prepared) later on if indeed things do go awry. For example, you have £350,000 to invest in a house. You have seen a house at auction, and a builder has given an estimate of £80,000 to make the repairs. You will need at least a 10 per cent contingency budget for that amount (£8,000) and you know that the auctioneer will charge 15 per cent for the sale. There are also your legal and moving fees. Your top bid, therefore, can realistically go no higher than £224,000 if you are to cover all the payments within your budget:

- ▶ Hammer **price**   £224,000
- ▶ Auctioneer's **tax**   £33,600
- ▶ **Repairs**   £80,000
- ▶ Contingency on **repairs** £8,000
- ▶ Total   £345,600

This leaves you £4,400 for legal and moving fees.

Try it now

Start now to look at your decisions from the perspective of risk. Think about the risk itself, how manageable it is, the probability of it happening, and how you deal with it if it occurs. The results could make the decision for you.

- ▶ Since risk is an important aspect of decision making, it is better managed than ignored.
- ▶ Think through the risks to your decision from as many angles as possible, and don't forget the links your decision may have to other factors.
- ▶ Start considering a contingency plan and budget for every decision you need to make. It will make the difference between you making a well-ordered decision or taking a gamble.
- ▶ Use the traffic light system when you want to categorize probability.
- ▶ Consider the identification of risk as being a way of making your final decision.

FOCUS POINTS

Chris has not thought about the risks of moving the financial staff out of the offices and expanding his workers into the new room; it just seemed like a good plan and a great way to solve a problem. He now realizes that he needs to think this through in a more structured way. The move will solve their immediate problem of space, and if the other company were to move out in six months' time Peters & Sons could take on their unit. However, what if it is just a rumour and the other company is not moving? He could end up with half a move that is insufficient for their needs and staff wondering what is going on. Moving offices and staff is expensive, especially if it is temporary, and Chris does not want to spend money on a move that might not give the company the outcome it wants. He decides that, as he invited his team to help him brainstorm ideas, there is an expectation now that something will happen, so he will get them together again, this time to help him assess all the risks and to consider acceptable contingency measures.

Pat is delighted about her staff's offer to accept low wages for the first two weeks, but a family friend in business has warned her to be careful about staff contracts: she cannot just pay staff half a wage because the salon is not yet bringing in a profit. She realizes that there is more to paying staff than she thought and that she might have to look up some employment law or speak to her accountant. However, she does not have time for that right now, so that option will have to go. She feels back to square one with regard to her funding problem – until the same family friend who advised her steps in and makes her an offer. She says that she will loan Pat 25 per cent of the initial start-up costs at a very low interest, in return for monthly payments and having her hair done every week in the salon for free. Although Pat thinks this is a good offer, as it would solve her problem, this time she decides to do a full risk analysis (including contingencies) on the offer *before* coming to a final decision. She is also aware that keeping information from the staff until she has made her decision will help to make them feel more settled and there will be less gossip.

Next Step

We have seen why assessing risk is important in decision making, and looked at how you can manage potential risk. However, some people love to make decisions 'on the hoof', so we will now see whether we can – or should – make some decisions quickly. Can we trust our gut reaction, or is that just lazy decision making?

5

Intuitive or rash?

Goal: To identify when a gut reaction is the right solution and the implications of taking this route to decision making.

Read the following statements about making quick decisions, and say how much you agree with them by circling one of the numbers. If you disagree with the statement circle the 1, if you neither agree nor disagree circle the 3, and if you fully agree circle the 5:

I like making quick decisions	1 2 3 4 5
I never regret a quick decision	1 2 3 4 5
I feel that making decisions 'on the hoof' makes me appear strong	1 2 3 4 5
I think that people who cannot make quick decisions are weak	1 2 3 4 5
I consider myself a decisive person	1 2 3 4 5
I have a preference for looking to the future, moving on	1 2 3 4 5
I don't like dwelling on things	1 2 3 4 5
I believe that the best answers are usually the first ones that come into your head	1 2 3 4 5
I see myself as a force for change	1 2 3 4 5
People come to me to make decisions for them	1 2 3 4 5
Now add up your score and put the total in the box. **Total score =**	

Score	Result
41–50	You are an amazing powerhouse for decision making, and you probably relate your ability to think fast and be decisive with being powerful and strong. This may be part of your job or something you have developed. However, you need to consider that, in acting fast, you may be missing certain data or other options. If you are a manager who is making decisions for others rather than helping them to make their own decisions, you may be fostering reliance instead of developing your staff to think for themselves. If this is you, you will need to consider the long-term implications of this.
26–40	In some situations – but not all – you may be fairly confident about making quick decisions. You see the necessity of making fast decisions, but may not always feel comfortable or confident about operating at such a speed; perhaps you have had your fingers burned once or twice. Some industries rely on fast decision making, but not everyone feels able to move at this pace.
Below 25	You really don't feel comfortable making decisions on the hop, and in some instances it may even scare you to do so. Perhaps you are in an industry or job that does not need that type of decision making or maybe you are a more reflective person. Does this fear get in the way of your performance in your job? You may be concerned about making quick decisions in your personal life, too. Not all decisions have to be made quickly, but you might like to think about how you could speed up some of your decisions.

Some decisions have to be made quickly, and rightly so. In an emergency we would not prepare a matrix or risk analysis; we would act as fast as possible from knowledge, instinct and intuition.

However, with the luxury of time, too much consideration can lead to the monster of decision making: procrastination. There is always a danger that through our careful deliberations we are actually subconsciously putting off that final decision. If this is you, you need to discover the ways in which you can make fast decisions.

To make a decision fast, there is no better way than flipping a coin – heads you do one thing, tails the other. How do you feel about that? Does it make you feel uncomfortable, because surely there was no real thought there? Or maybe it makes you feel pleased that a decision has been made, whatever the outcome. First of all, let's debunk some of the mystery that surrounds fast decision making.

Remember this: Fast decisions can be easy

Anyone can make a fast decision – just say the first option that comes into your head. Yes or no. There is nothing clever or talented about this; young children are particularly good at it because they are unhampered by any thoughts of repercussions. Separate out the decision from the implications and you will see that making the actual decision is very simple.

The mystery of decision making

Like so many mysteries, there is usually something quite ordinary behind the mystery itself, some simple explanation that, if it were known, would burst the bubble. Even if you are a measured and systematic thinker, there will have been times when you have had to make a quick decision.

Try it now

Think about some of the ways in which you have made quick decisions. Have you ever flipped a coin or tossed two sticks in a stream and bet on which one would appear on the other side of the bridge first? If so, was that decision any better or worse than one that you stewed over for hours?

We all know people who make decisions in this fast and easy way, and perhaps we even envy them a little. After all, they seem so decisive. But if we take the example of flipping a coin, there are two possible outcomes so the probability of getting it correct is 50:50, which means the odds of getting it wrong are not very high.

We also see this in action when someone tries to predict the gender of an unborn child. There will be calls of 'It's definitely a boy' and, equally, 'I know it's a girl, I can sense it.' Even if they use the old trick of a wedding ring suspended from a thread, there still remains the point that you have high odds of getting it right, as the baby is sure to be either a boy or a girl. In other words, you have an even chance of being right. However, something interesting happens after the revelation. Those who selected the right gender, upon hearing that they are correct, will seek to confirm that it is not a guess or chance but some form of talent they have. You will hear them saying, 'I was right, it's a girl, I have never been wrong yet,' and even saying, 'It is a gift I have.'

However, those that have been proved to be incorrect will often seek to:

▸ deny it – 'I don't think it was me that thought it was a boy. I think you might be muddling me up with someone else.'

▸ change their story – 'Yes, I thought it was a boy initially but I changed that to a girl about two weeks ago. I'm sure I told you that.'

▸ avoid it – 'I don't think I took part in that. Was I even in the office that day?'

▸ accept it, but with a proviso – 'I can't understand it, I am usually 100 per cent right; this is the first time *ever* I have got this wrong.'

These are common responses and you may recognize yourself in one of them, or you may even have thought of more. The point here is that we have an inbuilt damage limitation mechanism that saves us from our own negative feelings about being wrong – even though the rational 'us' knows that there was a 50 per cent chance that we would have guessed wrong anyway.

So people who are able to make fast, decisive decisions are not necessarily imbued with any particular talent for getting it right. If they have any talent at all, it is in their ability to find a way out of explaining how they were actually wrong. We will be looking at ways in which you can deal with getting it wrong later in the chapter, but at this point it is important to note that fast decision makers are simply that – they make the decision *fast*, irrespective of the outcome.

Our biggest fear in decision making is that we make the wrong decision, but in many situations it is almost impossible to know whether you took the right decision or not because you cannot turn back the clock (remember the 5th rule of decision making described in the introduction). For example, you are torn between two houses that you like. You make a selection, but shortly afterwards things seem to go wrong in your life. Your first thought is, what would have happened if I had bought the other property? Would that have brought me more luck? Would this not have happened to me if I had moved there instead?

> **Key idea: You cannot turn the clock back**
> The truth, in the scenario above, is that you will never know. Perhaps if you had bought the other house, something worse might have happened. We cannot know how life might have panned out for us if we had made other choices and, therefore, unless there is actual proof of a connection, there is no point in agonizing about past decisions.

When and how to make a fast decision

Are there any situations when it is more advantageous to make a fast decision? They are probably those when, if you don't, you worry that you will miss out. However, beware; this is a ploy often used by salespeople. We have all heard things like, 'The 20 per cent discount is only for people who sign up now.' Unless you had already decided that you wanted the item (in which case it is a good deal), it pays to be wary of this type of inducement. It is designed to push the person on the verge of purchasing the product over the edge and into buying it – and, furthermore, make them feel good about their purchase (after all, it was on offer).

> **Remember this: Think before you act**
> If you ever have this experience, take a moment to go back in your mind. Before you became embroiled in this situation, were you actively looking for this product? Was it something you really wanted? If so, then go ahead, but if not, it is better to announce the fact that you would like to delay. It is highly unlikely that a reputable company would ever try to push you into a deal there and then, or that the offer will not be available later that day, when you have had time to think about it a little more.

Another consideration for making fast decisions is the level of risk you – or your company – are willing to take (a subject we explored in the previous chapter). It used to be thought that men were quicker at assessing the level of risk and therefore made faster decisions than women (and they were therefore more suited to management) but that is not generally considered the case today. Anyone can make fast decisions if they decide to do so.

Consider these two decisions:

1 Changes need to be made to the contract for a £1 million project to go ahead. The other party needs to meet on Tuesday but you have other work scheduled in the next few days for other customers, and they are important, too. You need to decide what to do.
2 One of your customers has not received a delivery. They are cross about the situation, as they need the goods urgently. You need to decide what to do.

Let's look at this from a risk point of view:

In the first situation the risk is very high. There cannot be many companies that could cope with losing a £1 million project, and therefore you decide that you must give this your priority. A quick decision based on risk would be to take the following actions:

▶ Agree the meeting for next Tuesday.
▶ Clear your calendar of less important meetings and tasks for the days up to the meeting. Any work that needs to be done in that time for other customers must either be delayed or delegated to others. This will free you up enough time to meet with your legal department to sort out the contract.

The second decision is annoying and upsetting but is not so high risk. Even if this customer is an important one, it is unlikely that this cannot be negotiated and one customer is rarely the ruination of a company, unless they are the main customer. Therefore a quick decision based on lower risk would be to take the following actions:

▶ Contact the customer and apologize.
▶ Offer either to have the products couriered over to them or a replacement sent in the usual way. Later on you can check how this situation occurred, but for now you could also offer the customer a voucher or refund option.

Key idea: Assess the risk
Assessing risk is a useful tool to help you make decisions quickly, and also provides some justification for the outcome you choose.

Tapping into your senses

You may now be thinking: what about intuition? Have you ever heard any of the following?

- ▶ 'I can feel it in my stomach when the decision is right.'
- ▶ 'I don't know why but I know I am right, I can feel that I am right.'
- ▶ 'I had a feeling that I should stay away from that deal, and I was right.'
- ▶ 'I had a gut feeling...'

We all like to think that we have senses that are finely tuned to help us stay away from danger (and that includes making bad decisions), and in many ways we are right. It is certainly not unusual to have a 'feeling' about something; we are basically mammals, after all, and so perhaps we should learn to listen to our 'gut feelings' more and rely on reason less.

It is true that some of us are more intuitive than others but that does not mean that there is no room for improvement. Tapping into our senses is not something that is always encouraged, especially at work where a formal approach to decision making is deemed more appropriate, probably because it can be audited and the decision traced back to its origin. However, that does not mean that we cannot use our intuition in certain circumstances.

We are all born intuitive as it is part of our survival mechanism, but as we come to rely on other systems, such as having someone feed us regularly, we lose our natural instincts. However, they can be revived and developed. For example, the sense of smell in babies is very strong. They can distinguish their own mothers from others by smell, but we lose some of this ability when other senses become more dominant. Animals can smell fear in others, and this is possibly also true of humans, although we may not recognize it.

Try it now

For just one hour, try to hone in on the smells of those around you. What are they telling you? Are the smells good or do they make you feel wary? Consider how reliant on smell you would be if you only had this sense on which to base your decisions.

Although you may never use intuition in the workplace to make significant decisions, acknowledge its place in making fast decisions in other areas of your life, and further develop your senses.

Unconscious intelligence

Are we born to be a fast or slow decision maker?

Which of these two statements best describes you?
'I like to make decisions fast – that's just the way I am.'
'I like to think for a while before making a decision – that's just the way I am.'

Most people would not find it difficult to come down in favour of one statement or the other. After all, they are polar opposites and one probably represents us more than the other. However, that does not mean they have to be mutually exclusive. In other words, you can decide to be both, in different circumstances.

Inevitably, we make some decisions very fast, such as which parking space to go for or when to apply the brakes in our car. Other decisions benefit from being more considered, such as what to choose for lunch from the vast display in a restaurant or which item of clothing to wear on a date. Therefore even if you think that, for most decisions, you are a 'statement 1' person, sometimes, for decisions with more choice, you may consider a little longer. Similarly, you may think that you are mostly a 'statement 2' person, but acknowledge that there are some occasions when you do have to be fairly decisive in a short amount of time.

Being able to change and flex your style is called having emotional intelligence, and is one of the main skills employers look for in staff today. Having emotional intelligence is being able to adapt your style to a given situation. This means that in some situations you will decide on a fast response, but in others you will decide that a longer decision period is more fitting and may lead to a better-quality outcome. This ability to decide on the most appropriate response in each circumstance does not always come naturally, and therefore we may need to overtly think about each situation. For example, when you answered the question at the beginning of this section (which of these two statements best describes you?), you probably responded instinctively, without thinking it through – and that is what I wanted you to do. Most of us respond in this way much of the time. To flex your emotional intelligence muscles, you will need to be more aware of those innate responses when you are asking yourself whether a course of action is the right one in a given situation.

Remember this: We all have automatic responses

If someone you meet in the street asks you how you are, you will probably say 'Fine', whether you are or not. That level of innate response is perfect for social situations but not in general life or for making business decisions. Think about how and where you respond automatically. Are your responses simply time-saving ones, and should you be paying more attention to the question?

Going with the group

Throughout this chapter I have been making the assumption that you are taking decisions alone, but of course in some instances you may decide or be asked to make a decision as a group. Some groups come to consensus very quickly but others do not, and if this is the case you could find yourself stuck in hours of negotiations.

In this situation all manner of dynamics may come into play. An example of this is the group ostracizing one person, in the hope that they feel so uncomfortable they leave (either mentally or physically). Another ploy is for the group to wear down the minority party so that they eventually give in to the majority view, just to get out of the room. If you are in a group decision situation, and not everyone appears to agree, watch out for this game play and other tactics.

In his studies of group conformity, the psychologist Solomon Asch noted another phenomenon. In one of his famous 1950s experiments, the group was made up of people recruited to say (falsely) that one of the lines printed on one card was equal in length to a line on another card, together with one volunteer who had been given no information. The volunteer did not know that the others had been primed to lie, but in most cases when the group members were asked to state their view about the length of the lines, the volunteer lied to give the same answer as the others. In other words, the individual preferred to conform to the group rather than stand alone, even though this meant giving an incorrect answer.

From this Asch concluded that people do not like to appear different from the group and will conform to the majority decision in many situations. The result of the study had huge implications for juries and other groups brought together to make crucial decisions. The decision you made that you thought felt intuitive at the time (after all, if everyone else made the same choice they must have felt it too, and if everyone feels like that then it must be right) is really a form of group manipulation. You may feel that it is quicker (and right) to go with the group decision, but is it really what you want?

Remember this: A group can be manipulative
When you are brought together in a group to make a decision, it's important to watch out for game play and not to feel pushed into making a decision you consider unsound. Instead, suggest a secret ballot to protect everyone and allow all to be honest.

Your moral compass

How well developed is your moral compass? It may seem old-fashioned to think of making decisions based on our own personal values, but there is no denying that having a moral framework to hand provides you with a fast and efficient decision-making tool.

Our moral outlook is based on many aspects of our life and how we live. How we are brought up and the boundaries we are given, and the examples of what is acceptable as demonstrated by others and the society we are living in, all fit together with our own thoughts on life and create a moral framework for how we live. For some, religion plays a huge role, and for others it is society, but whatever it is for you, these teachings not only help us lead our lives in an acceptable manner but also enable us to make decisions based on their rules.

For example, most people would think that stealing is morally wrong, so if I asked you to stand in front of me while I stole something from a shop, you would probably say 'No' straight away. Your moral compass has made the decision for you, and very fast too. Now switch that scenario to a work situation where someone is asking you to sign off expenses that you know are not real. That is stealing from the company, and you would do well to listen to that moral compass once again.

The moral compass not only makes the decision for us but it also provides us with an unbeatable reply. If someone asks you why you will not do the thing they are asking, you simply reply, 'Because I believe it to be morally wrong.' You cannot be blamed for your beliefs, and there really is no answer to that!

Remember this: Our moral compass can make our decision for us
We all know when some things are wrong, or make us feel uncomfortable. You are going to need to live with your decisions and therefore if you need to take a moral stand, do so; otherwise you may regret the outcome.

If it all goes wrong...

Earlier in the chapter I alluded to the fact that even fast decision makers make mistakes from time to time. In other words, they will make a decision that they (or someone) deem to be the wrong decision, even if they would have come to the same conclusion if they had decided more slowly. Often the other person is simply looking for a scapegoat or someone to blame for the outcome so that they can deflect it away from themselves, even if they were the one that took the decision forward.

When this happens, it is essential (unless you really have made a complete mess of things) that you are able to reassert yourself and maintain your self-esteem. Preserving your ego is hugely important if you are to go on in business and not suffer a crisis of confidence. Politicians are excellent at bouncing back from criticism, and therefore they are good to observe in this respect. However, having some good phrases to hand is always useful. For example:

- ▶ 'I made the best decision I could, given the information I had at the time.'
- ▶ 'Hindsight is a wonderful thing.'
- ▶ 'I had to make a fast decision and I did not notice anyone else coming forward.'
- ▶ 'I wanted to make a collective decision but everyone else disappeared.'
- ▶ 'Leadership does not come with a cast-iron guarantee of success.'
- ▶ 'I still think the decision was the right course of action, it is just that time has moved on and the details have changed.'

▶ 'I don't want to talk about mistakes, I want to discuss what we have learned from this.'

Key idea: Quick decisions are perceived as riskier

All decisions carry some form of risk, but quick decisions are perceived as riskier than ones that take longer because they may appear rash and ill-considered. This is not always true but they carry that additional criticism, as if the speed alone justified the outcome. Always ensure that you have some solid retort to restore your self-esteem and authority.

FOCUS POINTS

▶ There is no mystery to fast decision making, and anyone can do it.

▶ Use the measure of risk as a way of making a quick decision.

▶ Choose how you want to make decisions, and be more aware and in control of your own actions.

▶ Some decisions need to you act with your heart and conscience rather than rationally and dispassionately.

▶ Make sure that you can justify your decision, however it was made.

Chris made a snap decision that moving into the offices nearby would be the right thing to do, but now he is wondering whether he was a little too hasty. He has not been a supervisor long, and he thinks it might have been better to work some things out first, before jumping. The problem is that he has now set up an expectation that this is what will happen, and only this morning one of the office workers came to see him because she was worried about a rumour that she would have to work from home. She said that she did not want to do that and did not have room for a computer workstation in her house. Chris spent 20 minutes calming her down and wondering if he was making decisions too quickly and openly. While he feels his decision to move some of the functions is basically sound, he needs to rethink which ones and how to go about it. He also feels that involving the team in helping with the decision was good, but he now needs to think carefully about how he does this, rather than acting rashly and regretting it later. Chris is thinking that sometimes he rushes too fast towards a solution without taking the time to think things through.

Pat has done her risk analysis and the offer seems a good one but, even so, she still wants to consider it further. Pat is used to making quick decisions in her work all the time. Which colour dye to give the customer the result they want, who should go to lunch first, how the holiday rota is actioned for fairness, whom to appoint and who is not working – all these decisions are everyday occurrences for Pat, but this decision feels very different. Pat recognizes that it is because it is high risk and carries with it a stream of implications for herself and the people she employs. Her intuition says 'take it' but she can't go to the bank and tell them that the decision is based on intuition. She needs more solid reasons. What should she do?

Next Step

This chapter looked at different techniques for making fast decisions. A flexible approach – a measure of emotional intelligence – offers the ability to either speed up or slow down your decision making to suit the situation. In the next chapter we will be doing just that, using models of more complex scenarios where a fast decision would not be appropriate.

6

Structured decision making

Goal: To look at a number of models for managing decisions in a structured way.

Self-assessment

Read the following statements about structured decision making, and say how much you agree with them by circling one of the numbers. If you disagree with a statement circle the 1, if you neither agree nor disagree circle the 3, and if you fully agree circle the 5:

I love working with models and frameworks	1 2 3 4 5
I like everything to be structured	1 2 3 4 5
I believe that working through a process liberates my mind	1 2 3 4 5
I gain comfort from knowing that someone else has designed a tried and tested process that I can use	1 2 3 4 5
I like to present my ideas through models and diagrams	1 2 3 4 5
I feel that using a model or process shares the blame if the decision is wrong	1 2 3 4 5
I like to work by sectioning items or processes out	1 2 3 4 5
I prefer to work incrementally	1 2 3 4 5
I think that when a decision has been proved to be incorrect, it should be easy to track it back	1 2 3 4 5

I believe that decisions should not be taken 'on the hoof'	1 2 3 4 5
Now add up your score and put the total in the box. **Total score =**	

Score	Result
41–50	You really like working with models, frameworks and processes. You probably feel uncomfortable making any large decision where you have not had enough time to consider every angle and the risks involved and weighed the possible outcomes. Structured decision making works well in business life but you probably also incorporate elements of it into your home life, too, perhaps when buying a home or organizing a family event such as a wedding.
26–40	You are fairly comfortable with both 'on the hoof' decision making and structured decision making. You can see the benefits (and drawbacks) of both, and you can use whichever approach is the most appropriate accordingly. You may like to think about how you use each style in your life, as there may be some occasions when you are using one type when the other may be more advantageous.
Below 25	You really are not keen on using structured decision making. This could be because you like to make decisions using your 'gut feeling' or because you are unsure of how to use a model for decision making, or even what it can do for you. If this is the case, then you should find this chapter enlightening.

In the previous chapter we looked at making quick, impetuous decisions. This did not mean that they were bad decisions, just that they were made fast, using intuition or instinct. I would now like to introduce you to another way of making decisions, using a structure or framework.

Why get caught up in structure?

You may be wondering why, if making decisions on the hoof is so easy and liberating, you would want to do anything else. After all, aren't quick thinkers and decisive people more valued than those who systematically go through a process, only to come out with what may be the same answer? Isn't the story of the tortoise and the hare just that? Surely everyone knows that the hare should really have won!

Well, that depends on the situation. Imagine that you go to the doctor, and as soon as you sit down and start to explain your symptoms, the doctor interrupts with, 'You have a bad cold, take this,' and hands you a prescription. You may be thinking, 'That was a bit quick. I haven't even mentioned my aching joints yet, or my double vision.' You would probably not be pleased with the doctor and feel that he/she had made a hasty diagnosis without even trying to find out about all your symptoms.

Of course, no doctor would actually do this. Instead, they will go through a process of asking specific questions that allow them to confirm or eliminate a diagnosis, so that they can differentiate meningitis from influenza or influenza from a heavy cold. This process of going through systematic questioning is a form of structured decision making that leads the doctor towards what should be the correct answer. The structure not only provides a template for ascertaining the condition but it also forms a good defence should the doctor get it wrong. After all, it is then the process that is at fault and not the doctor.

It would be the same if you took your car into a garage because it was making a strange clunking sound. Again, you would not be very happy if the technician simply looked at the car and tried to guess what the problem could be. You would at least expect them to go through some form of diagnostic test, whether that was using electronics, a practical test, or just asking you questions, to ensure that the conclusion they come to is the correct one.

These are just two illustrations to help you understand how structured decision making can help us, and why we should consider using it in some situations. Reaching a decision by going through a structured process enables us to:

▶ think through the process in logical steps
▶ ensure that we have remembered to look at all aspects of the problem and not forgotten anything
▶ consider any 'outside' or accompanying issues (such as impact on other areas of work)
▶ emerge with a credible decision that stands up to scrutiny.

The beautiful decision

Ah, the decision! It is great when it all works out, but at this point, for now, I want to separate the decision from the process – and I have my reasons for taking you down this route.

I have already said that a structured decision is a logical way of making a decision, but it does not guarantee you the outcome you want. For example, I was recently with a group who wanted to decide where to have their Christmas lunch. They told me that it could be anywhere except The White Horse because they did not want to go there.

We started off by listing the venues they liked across the top of a sheet of paper like this:

| Gulliver's | The Shamrat | The Pavilion | The White Horse |

As you can see, I included The White Horse because I felt it should be in there as it was indeed a possible option. Not wanting it is not a sufficient reason not to include it, especially as they could not explain why they did not want to go there.

Now we needed some criteria to help us make the decision. I asked the group what the key things were that were required and they came up with the following:

- ▶ free parking outside
- ▶ vegetarian option available
- ▶ traditional Christmas dinner
- ▶ less than five miles away
- ▶ able to provide the dinner after 2 p.m.
- ▶ no restriction on time.

Having confirmed that this was the full list of criteria, we then marked each venue against the criteria, like this:

Criteria	Gulliver's	The Shamrat	The Pavilion	The White Horse
Free parking outside	✓		✓	✓
Vegetarian option available	✓	✓	✓	✓
Traditional Christmas dinner	✓		✓	✓
Less than five miles away	✓	✓	✓	✓
Able to provide the dinner after 2 p.m.		✓		✓
No restriction on time		✓		✓

As you can see from the grid, only The White Horse could meet all the criteria, and therefore the decision matrix was saying that they should select this option. 'But we said we didn't want The White Horse!' they complained. 'What a rubbish decision-making tool!' Herein lies the rub: the decision-making tool is not at fault. It is a perfectly good way of structuring a decision, the decision is fine, in fact it is a beautiful decision – it is just the answer they did not like.

Notice that I clarified their criteria for the decision before filling in the responses, and so there was no good reason why they should not use The White Horse, since it met all their criteria. 'I don't like it' was not given as a criterion for deciding.

The point I am making here is when using a structured form of decision making like this, it is hugely important to acknowledge that you may not like the result. It is a process and you need to be dispassionate about the outcome.

To take another example, many people may write a list of wants for their next house that looks somewhat like this:

▶ must have at least three bedrooms
▶ must have a large, square kitchen
▶ must have a study area or spare room downstairs.

They then go and fall in love with a tiny two-bedroom cottage that has none of these things. This is fine if you are free to follow your heart, but a distinct problem if you are following a decision matrix to help you make a rational, justifiable decision.

Remember this: The criteria must be robust

You must not try to manipulate your matrix by attempting to include criteria that give you the decision you want, in an effort to swing the matrix into favouring your pre-chosen outcome. If you do this, the tool will not be objective enough to be a robust decision-making instrument.

Going for consensus

There is no rule that says that decisions have to be taken in isolation. They can just as easily be managed within a group. There are significant benefits to this, in that:

▶ the responsibility for the decision is shared
▶ any risks are also shared
▶ more brains around the table can result in more ideas
▶ a greater number of people will buy into the decision and claim it as their own.

Consensus is when everyone agrees on a decision. For some people it is the obvious answer to decision making and for others the Holy Grail – a great idea but not really attainable. For this reason, and before starting, it is important to identify where consensus would be valuable and where it could be difficult.

Consensus is helpful wherever you have a decision that needs everyone to 'buy in' to the outcome, for example, a meeting to decide on the care plan for an elderly person, or how a child should be looked after. It can also be used to share risk, as seen in the jury system where everyone needs to agree before a certain outcome can be unanimous or upheld.

The very act of consensus brings to bear other skills, such as negotiating and persuading skills in addition to all manner of 'people skills'. Where people disagree it requires everyone to communicate, share their feelings and explain why they feel their outcome is the right choice. When this process works successfully, it can result in a strong team that has bonded over the decision.

However, there are occasions when consensus is not appropriate. For example, most immediate or emergency situations would not work with consensus. Where a situation needs someone to step forward, show leadership and take a firm decision or some decisive action, trying to gain consensus would slow everything down and may introduce barriers that you do not need.

Remember this: Consensus may be inappropriate
Consensus decision making is great for engaging and involving everyone, listening to their views and reaching a joint decision – but it is not helpful in an emergency or when a decision needs one strong leader.

Focus groups

A focus group is a number of people brought together to help provide an organization with more information and help them make a decision. Many years ago I was invited to be in a focus group to decide on the design and decoration of a proposed new local restaurant. The focus group was made up of the type and age of its intended customers and it was our job to debate what we liked and disliked about each of the proposed designs once the architect had left the room.

Three themes had been selected and each concept was presented by the architect who designed it. At the end of the session we had to vote for the design that we felt would be the most successful in the town, and also the one that we would personally use. The final decision for the style of the restaurant still lay with the restaurant owners, but they now had so much more additional information and views from potential customers to help them.

Many focus groups today are filmed so that the behaviour of the group can also be taken into consideration. This is to ensure that everyone contributes and that no one person is overbearing with their views. The psychologists will also watch out for body language and look for the game play, mentioned previously, that sometimes occurs in groups.

Focus groups are often used in marketing, when it needs to be decided whether a new product is viable. By asking people to comment in a controlled environment the company can eliminate some products and ascertain which ones will go forward to further development and then eventually make it on to the shelves.

Focus groups have some similarity to learning sets, mentioned previously, as they both bring together a group to help make a decision. In learning sets it is helpful for the group to be made up of people from different backgrounds, while focus groups usually comprise people deemed to come from a certain category, such as a specific age group, or types of people who would use the proposed restaurant.

Introducing a simple grid

A two-dimensional grid can help you visualize where you should be spending your time and can help with many decisions. Let's imagine that you own a small farm shop, selling eggs, fruit and vegetables. Business has been slow lately and you have been thinking of diversifying. As the business is quiet you have some extra time available, but you have to stay on the premises as you cannot yet afford to employ anyone else. After thinking through some suggestions, you decide that several avenues are open to you. For example, you could:

- ▶ increase your range to include local crafts
- ▶ make some crafts yourself to sell
- ▶ learn floristry and move into producing posies and bouquets
- ▶ rent out some of your space to another local business.

Our criteria for selection are, firstly, speed of implementation (because the business cannot survive much longer with low sales) and, secondly, low cost (because we cannot afford much investment at this stage).

Looking at our list, we can make the following table:

Increase range to include local crafts	Fast implementation, low cost
Make some crafts to sell	Medium implementation, medium cost
Learn floristry and move into producing posies and bouquets	Slow implementation, high cost
Rent out some space to another business	Fast implementation, low cost

Placed on an axis they look like this:

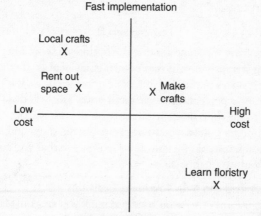

From this we can see that the two main contenders are increasing your range to include local crafts and renting out some space to another business. It may be that you can do both of these things, but if you had to select one option to try you might return to the grid again but this time with two different criteria axis. This time we will look at how they fare against long-term fit with the business (because you can't start something and then stop when your other business picks up) and flexibility (because we don't want to make too much commitment just in case the other business suddenly takes off). Given these two criteria, we now have:

Increase range to include local crafts	High long-term fit, high flexibility
Rent out some space to another business	Low long-term fit, low flexibility

Once again on an axis, they look like this:

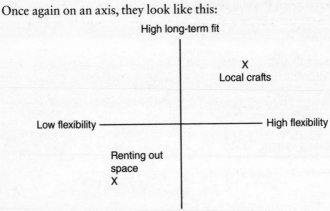

You can see from this diagram that the option we should be considering seriously now is that of attracting local craft sellers to display their wares in the shop on a sale or return basis, with the shop retaining a percentage of the retail price. This will draw more customers to the shop (and introduce them to your wares), bring in additional income, allow you to be present in the shop, and should this situation not work, then there is flexibility in that you could return to your original business.

Key idea: A grid can help you make decisions

You can use any criteria on your grid but if you are going to layer your criteria (because each grid can only handle two criteria at a time), you must start with your most important criteria first, and then work from there, refining with each further grid.

Feeling the weight

If you feel that setting out ideas on a grid is not for you, how about weighting certain options? The weight is the extent to which we feel they meet the criteria, when weighed against the other options.

You can give options weight depending on their merits and then, in some instances where the figures are the same, some options may even cancel each other out. Let's take the example used in the previous grid and weigh the options against one another. Here I have used percentages but you could give scores out of 10 or 100 instead. It does not matter as long as you use the same measure to make a comparison.

The first two criteria were speed of implementation against cost, and might look like this:

	Weight for quick implementation	Weight for low cost
Increase range to include local crafts	80%	80%
Make some crafts to sell	20%	30%
Learn floristry and move into producing posies and bouquets	20%	45%
Rent out some space to another business	75%	85%

In the example above we can see that some options automatically hold more weight than others, and that given this scenario you would also select increasing your range to include local crafts and renting out some space as being the most obvious contenders. Running them further through the weighting options again would look like this:

	Weight for business fit	Weight for flexibility
Increase your range to include local crafts	75%	85%
Rent out some of your space to another business	15%	20%

You would therefore still have come to the same conclusion.

Remember this: Weighting will score your options
When using weighting techniques, you need to be honest as you are setting your own criteria and percentages and it would be easy to 'fix' the results if you wanted a specific outcome.

A game of consequences

Try it now

Think of a recent decision you made. What impact did it have on others? Did you find that your decision affected no one but yourself, or did you find that it was like dropping a pebble into a pond, the ripples spreading out and affecting other people and situations?

Later in the book we will discuss again how decisions can have an impact on others, but in this section I want us to use that information in a different way, as a way of making the decision. How many times has someone said to you, 'If only I had known beforehand that they would have been upset, I would never have done it'? The truth is that we rarely think through all the consequences of our decisions. Naturally, we cannot think of the consequences of everything, otherwise we would never make it out of bed each morning, but when it comes to important decisions, perhaps a little more thought is needed. We can use this focus on consequences to help us make that essential decision.

As an example of how to do this, suppose you want to decide whether to buy a new car or a second-hand one this time. Grab yourself a large piece of paper and draw two bubble shapes in the centre. Within the first bubble, write 'new car' and in the second bubble write 'second-hand car'. Now, draw lines from the bubble outwards, detailing the consequences of each. For example, some of the consequences of buying a new car may be:

- ▶ need to find the finance
- ▶ no holiday next year
- ▶ Mum won't like me doing this
- ▶ taking on a loan
- ▶ will help with my ego!

Some of the consequences of buying a second-hand car may be:

- ▶ I can go on a summer holiday
- ▶ it might need replacing in two years
- ▶ it keeps Mum happy
- ▶ I won't need a loan.

As you can see, some of these consequences are positive and some are negative. Looking at consequences will not shortcut you to a decision but it will force you to be real about the two options, and not hide any of the factors. There is also something powerful about the act of writing things down. It can help you order your thoughts and also face some difficult aspects of the situation that perhaps you would have rather not thought about. Whatever your decision, if there is some other consequence that you had not considered, then it will be truly remarkable, as you will have explored the subject from all known angles.

Key idea: An honest decision needs careful thought

So many of our decisions are clouded by emotion and what we want that it is easy to fool ourselves that we could never have seen that consequence, but of course that is not always true. This activity will enable you to project forward and analyse the possible outcomes of your actions. You should then be able to make an honest decision based on careful thought.

Winners and losers

In the activity above we looked at the consequences of two decisions, but some decisions require there to be winners and losers as part of that outcome. You can assess this by doing a stakeholder analysis.

Try it now

In the example of buying a new car in the section above you can see that 'Mum' was a clear stakeholder because she was considered an important factor in the decision of whether or not to go ahead. Think of others who might have been important in the decision, such as the person's partner and the car salesperson.

Stakeholders are people who hold a stake in a decision. For example, shareholders are stakeholders in a company and would want to be involved in any decision that the company makes because they have a vested interest in it. Parents are stakeholders in the school that their children attend, because even though they don't attend themselves, again they have an interest in the way in which the school operates and makes decisions. There may even be a need for them to be involved in the decision making itself.

Creating a stakeholder analysis can therefore help us to make a decision by enabling us to think about who else stands to win or lose, and their level of involvement. It can also help us formulate other strategies for future negotiations. For example, when a school considers its stakeholders it will see who has most to win or lose in any decision and then put in place a number of substitute ideas to try to appease all parties.

> **Key idea: Some decisions are a compromise**
>
> Imagine that you had to decide whether to renovate the old school vegetable plot or create a new play area on the site. Some parents will want the first option and others the second. However, when you look at the stakeholders and why they would want each option you can begin to formulate ideas for compromise, so that even those who lose have been heard and their idea perhaps addressed in another way. It may or may not lead to a clear decision, but it can help you to gauge the depth of feeling and manage and tailor your response.

Stakeholders are hugely important because if they don't like your decision they can be disruptive. Get them on your side and they will be similarly supportive and will back your decision to the end. Identifying them can help you to make the initial decision, create a strategy around the decision and then work with them to support the outcome. In an example like the one above it is essential to know how people feel about a proposed decision like this, rather than just resting the decision on your own judgement.

Making it happen

All decisions need a point at which action is required. The decision itself is rarely an end in itself but quite often we believe that it is. How many times have you thought, 'I just need to make this decision and then I'm done,' and then found that the decision on its own was not sufficient to change anything – it needed to be implemented in some way.

Unless you are making a decision on which lottery numbers to choose, it is highly likely that you will need to take action following your decisive outcome. Start by 'chunking up' the task into a number of actions and set deadlines or targets for achieving each action, or delegate them to others. Being a person who is good at decision making is rarely all about the decision – it includes the follow through. In other words, good decision makers are also described as people who make things happen, go-getters and leaders. That's not bad for mastering a skill that anyone can learn.

***

Remember this: All decisions need an action

Quite often, reaching a decision is only impressive if it is followed up by smart action, so be firm and clear and get started on making it happen!

***

FOCUS POINTS

▶ A structured decision-making tool can help you make clear, justifiable decisions.

▶ If you have an outcome in mind that you favour – or don't favour – be open about it from the beginning.

▶ Use analysis of stakeholders and consequences to fully appreciate the implications of the outcome of every decision.

▶ Try out the structured tools to see how they work in different situations.

▶ A decision is not always an end it itself – it often needs action to make it happen.

Chris has been giving some quality thinking to the changes, and now thinks that this is not just about his ideas. He was right to include the staff but he feels that he may have become a little carried away with the feeling of importance it gave him. Whatever he decides will have to be agreed by the Peters family and his random thoughts do not look as good as a structured approach. Chris takes the problem to his supervisors' class and discusses it with his lecturer. His lecturer shows him how he was right to include the staff and to get as many ideas as possible, but agrees that he now needs a structured approach to back up his final decision. She shows him a couple of models and explains how they can be used within a business context, and Chris feels much more confident.

CASE STUDIES

Pat's offer has come from within her family and she feels that she should take it, but wants a further indication that she is doing the right thing. She decides to do a stakeholder analysis so that she can factor in her whole family and also manage their expectations. Pat has seven nieces and nephews and she realizes from the stakeholder analysis that she needs to set boundaries: for example, no dropping in for a free haircut every week! Through doing the analysis, Pat realizes that the stakeholders are not just herself and her family but also her staff and customers. She needs to consider them in her thoughts, too. They have been loyal and she needs to keep them – they all have an interest in seeing her succeed. Although Pat has already made her decision, she uses the stakeholder analysis to confirm that it is the right one.

Next Step

This chapter has shown you how structured methods can help you make decisions in a way that is credible and stands up to scrutiny. Many business decisions have to be like this because they may need to be tracked back and audited. For this reason we are next going to look at how to handle a range of business decisions.

7

Business-related decisions

Goal: To be able to make balanced decisions that enhance your business.

Read the following statements about making business-related decisions, and say how much you agree with them by circling one of the numbers. If you disagree with a statement circle the 1, if you neither agree nor disagree circle the 3, and if you fully agree circle the 5:

I am required to make business decisions at work	1 2 3 4 5
I feel confident about making business decisions	1 2 3 4 5
I like being responsible for making business decisions	1 2 3 4 5
I have never made a bad decision at work	1 2 3 4 5
Everyone in the team brings their decisions to me to make	1 2 3 4 5
I like to make decisions alone	1 2 3 4 5
I feel frustrated when other people try to help me make decisions	1 2 3 4 5
My boss or manager is totally happy with the way I make decisions	1 2 3 4 5
I see myself as a leader	1 2 3 4 5
I want promotion	1 2 3 4 5
Now add up your score and put the total in the box. **Total score =**	

Score	Result
41–50	You are very confident at making decisions and do not balk at making decisions alone; in fact, you may prefer it. You are keen to progress in your career and have identified decision making as a key skill for the future, and you would be right. However, consider whether you really need to make all those decisions alone. Could it be that you should be including others, or that others are feeling excluded from your team and are not always supportive of you?
26–40	You are fairly confident in your decision-making skills at work. You probably involve others where you need to and recognize that decision making is a balance. Not every decision has to be made solely by you, and sometimes sharing the risk and the task can bring teams together. Although decision making is a key skill for any manager, the real skill is undertaking it in the right way, and taking people with you.
Below 25	You may lack confidence, or perhaps your role does not currently involve much decision making. Much of the pay given to senior grades at work is directly correlated to the amount of decision making (and therefore risk to the company) that they handle. If you want to move forward in your career, you will therefore need to develop further in this area, and this chapter will give you some guidance and tips for making good business-related decisions.

Why are decisions at work different? A major reason is that they can carry so much weight and can even determine your career. If you make a hopeless decision at home the family may remember it, but the ramifications of making a poor decision at work may be that you lose more than just your friends.

The world of work can be at the same time both supportive and cut-throat, and in some organizations competition is encouraged. In that environment, losing is just not an option, so let's visit some of the most popular areas of decision making at work and discuss a better way forward.

If you want to move into management, decision making is a key skill and one that you will be using regularly. You cannot always hope to make the right decision every time but you can make your decision *in the right way* every time.

Remember this: A business decision needs to be made in the right way
With a work-based decision, how you make the decision can be more important than the outcome.

Business strategy and decision making

Business strategy is setting a path for the future, and the great thing about it is that you do not have to follow that same path if market forces change. For example, no one foresaw the recent economic downturn and therefore the future strategy of many companies has been forced to change. Organizations are now downsizing, focusing on their key products and even, in some cases, diversifying into completely new markets. Fascinating and exciting as this maybe, I'm sure that in many cases these moves were not decisions based on the strategic direction of the company three years ago.

Creating a business strategy is about looking to the future and envisioning the business in five to ten years' time. What will the business look like at that point? What will have fallen by the wayside? What will we hold dear? How do we see our business market developing and how can we position ourselves for a piece of that action? Are we too big? Are we too small? Do we need to focus more in one area or, conversely, divide our business over a greater number of areas?

> **Key idea: Build in flexibility**
>
> If you are in the position of making strategic decisions, you will be looking to the future as a guide to your business planning, but you must build in flexibility in case the future you predict is not the one that develops.

All businesses need a strategy, and this can aid decision making. For example, imagine that you work for a small-scale sweet manufacturer who sells only in this country, but their five year strategy includes the desire to break into the international sweet market. This strategy can help you to make decisions. When you are asked by the head of sales whether you will invest in a pitch at an international sweet fair, you would automatically know that this supports the company strategy, and if the money is available, I am sure you would say yes. Even if no orders emanate from the fair, the decision to exhibit can be justified, as it fits the company's long-term strategy, and if you want to be viewed as an international brand, you have to be seen in the right places. (If the strategy had been to remain within local markets, you would have decided to refuse the request, as it could not be described as a justified expense.)

Try it now

If you don't know your organization's long-term strategy, find out now. You will find information in the business plan or by speaking with management. You may find the information useful as it can help you guide your decisions towards the path that the organization is treading, even if others are not aware of it yet – and if the strategy changes, be prepared to change your decisions to reflect the new direction.

Operational decisions

Strategic decisions shape the future of a company but most of us deal with operational decisions all day, every day. These are the decisions that enable us to do day-to-day business and enable work to flow through the company. One minute we may be deciding which member of staff should be doing each job and the next deciding whether to order more materials now or wait until the end of the month.

Operational decisions are usually about resources. Among these could be:

▶ money
▶ people
▶ information and knowledge
▶ time
▶ materials
▶ products.

When needing to make decisions regarding these resources it is helpful to remember the triangle:

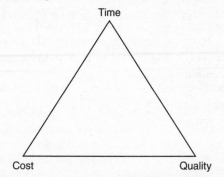

These are the three areas where you can make adjustments but that may have an impact on the other areas. For example, you could cut back on time, but it may cost you more and you may lose some of the quality. Conversely you may decide that cost is the main issue, in which case things may take a little longer and the quality is lost. Finally you may decide that the main focus must be quality, and that may cost more and take more time. Depending on the type of business you are involved in, there are areas of business where you pay a higher price for speed and others where you pay a high price for a longer period of time.

When making operational decisions, refer back to the structured techniques shown in Chapter 6. It is essential that the decision:

▶ demonstrates a train of thought and will hold up to scrutiny, and so keep notes
▶ is fair and honest (no favouritism)
▶ is legal
▶ supports both the company and any staff member involved
▶ is as unbiased as possible.

Decisions in meetings

Meetings are great places for making decisions, but two problems can occur: you are required to think on your feet (and not everyone excels at that) and you may also be influenced by the others in the meeting.

PRESSURE AND SPEED

When you have a group of people looking at you as a leader and expecting a decision, it is easy to feel pressurized into conforming. Unfortunately not everyone has razor-sharp powers of thought, and many people are reflectors, who need to mull over ideas and suggestions until they feel able to make that final decision. Naturally, some decisions to have to be made quickly but try never to feel pressured into making a decision on a whim.

THE GROUP

As pointed out earlier in this book, groups have amazing power to influence others, even when we are aware of it. When you feel pushed in one direction by the group in a meeting, ask for more time to consider. If it is a business meeting, suggest a coffee break or a make an excuse such as, 'I just need to clear my head a moment. Can we just take five minutes?' No one is going to refuse that request and it can just break the pressure that has been building up, allowing you to think more clearly.

Another aspect of making decisions in meetings is that you can share the decision and its outcome. For example, if you were to object to a house being built on some land, you may find yourself a target of hate mail or the recipient of bad feelings. However, if the same decision was made during a meeting and everyone agreed to the same outcome, it is more difficult to be an individual target, and the outcome appears to be more legitimate (after all, it was not just one person's view, everyone obviously felt the same way).

Remember this: Meetings come with their own problems
Meetings can be great forums for decisions but they come with their own problems and issues of which you need to be aware. They can make decision making either difficult or easier, depending on the way they are used.

Negotiating decisions

During a negotiation, decision making comes thick and fast. You have to be nimble in your thinking, but this is a skill that anyone can learn, and the secret to making good decisions in the negotiating arena is forward planning. If you enter a negotiation without having undertaken any planning, you are bound to be caught out and you run the risk of your decisions being snap decisions. That inevitably means you are back to flipping a coin or rolling a dice again, and while some people love the adrenalin rush of this, for many it feels as if they are out of control (and lack of planning will not be well received by your managers).

Remember this: Planning is essential
Planning is the answer to making great negotiating decisions. A few minutes of planning can save time in the actual meeting and make you feel more in control (which will radiate as confidence).

When we enter the workplace negotiating field, we know that ideally we want to leave with a win:win situation. That means that both sides gain in some way from the negotiation. This is why it is vital for both parties to establish and maintain a good relationship. Forcing the other person down (I win:you lose) is to be avoided: it is not good business practice because it causes resentment, which will make it difficult to work with the other party again in the future. Therefore you should be looking for an outcome where you can move the situation forward, with both sides gaining something from the negotiation.

Start your preparation by making a list. Mark up a piece of paper into two columns. Head the first with 'My desired outcome' and the second with 'Their desired outcome' and write in each column what you would like out of the negotiation. While you will be aware of all your own desired outcomes, you will probably be less aware of theirs, but if you give some thought to what you would want if you were in their position, there will be some obvious things you can note down. Try also to think beyond these points to whether they could have any hidden agendas of which you are not initially aware.

Now create another list by marking up another sheet of paper into three columns. Head the first one 'Must haves' and the second 'Concessions' and the third 'Negotiable'. Under the first column, write the outcomes that you really must have to ensure that you walk away from the negotiation with the basics in place. In the second column, list the aspects of the issue that you could give up. They are the areas that you may initially say you want, but that actually you could give up if you had to, especially if you are able to exchange them for some other advantage.

In the third column, list the factors that give you prime negotiation power. These are the points on which you can negotiate to ensure that you achieve all your 'Must haves'. Now look back at your first list. If you achieve all your 'Must haves', will that deliver your desired outcome? Check that all the items or aspects of the negotiation are in place. Now you have a useful document that you can take into the negotiation and use when it comes to making decisions. You have already done all the thinking and it just remains for you to keep your cool and refer to your paperwork from time to time, to make sure you are on track.

Decision making and teams

Teams that work together well also need to share decision making. It is tempting to think that strong leadership means always being the one to make the decisions, but in fact strong leadership is taking people with you, and that can be achieved through shared decision making.

Involving others in your decision making does not mean that you are unable to make the decision alone; it just shows that you value the input of others. Most people would agree that they are not the sole fount of all knowledge and that input from other sources can bring richness to ideas and result in a better outcome.

When you want to involve your team in a decision, use the following five-step plan:

1 Lay the idea or decision before them.
2 Explain why you would like their input, and reiterate that although you would like their help to explore the options and discuss all aspects, the final decision is yours.
3 Create some ground rules for working together (such as not talking over others, or not putting down anyone else's ideas).
4 Facilitate the group discussion, using any of the structured decision-making tools such as brainstorming or acting as a focus group if that is helpful.
5 Summarize your findings, thank the group, and explain to everyone involved how you intend to take this forward.

Key idea: Involving the team will increase ownership
Involving your team in making decisions can be hugely bonding for you and the team. Everyone will feel more involved right from the beginning, and they will have greater psychological investment in the outcome.

Recruitment decisions

When you are recruiting for a job, it is good to have a number of well-qualified people who answered your advertisement, but now you have to decide who the successful candidate should be. Your human resources department or officer may take on the initial shifting, leaving you with a shortlist of around six final candidates, but if you do not have that facility you will have to do everything yourself.

SHORTLISTING

When undertaking the initial stage – going through CVs or application forms and shortlisting – you will need to go through the following steps:

1 Arm yourself with a copy of the job description (JD) and/or person specification (PS).
2 Make a list of the key skills, knowledge and experience required for the job.
3 Mark each candidate on whether their CV or application form demonstrates that they meet the requirements of the job (do not

be sidetracked by names, addresses or 'impressive' skills such as being bilingual that were not specified for the job and are therefore not needed).

4 Select the candidates that best meet your requirements and invite them to interview.

5 Send a standard letter to those who did not meet the criteria.

INTERVIEWING

During each interview you will need to be as impartial and as fair as possible. Some people put amazing things on their CV or application form that you realize are clearly false when you interview them. Others do not do themselves justice. Your job is to ensure that everyone you see takes part in a fair process and has every opportunity to demonstrate their skills.

To make the decision a fair one, use a matrix with the candidates' names on one axis and the skills they need to exhibit or demonstrate on the other axis. Now set a score you feel able to work with, such as marks out of 20 or 100, and rate each person throughout the interview. For example, if the job required typing at 60 words per minute (wpm) and Leona Smith could do 30 wpm you might score her as 10 for that particular criterion, whereas Joe Brown might score 18 with his 50 wpm. Scoring like this can be subjective, however, so to make the process even fairer it is helpful to have a colleague undertaking the same activity. You can then compare results.

SELECTION

At the end of each interview, add up the number of points each candidate scored. This should make your decision for you. If there is no clear winner – you have two candidates with the same top score – look closely at where they made their scores, as this is likely to vary. Some aspects of the job will be more important than others, and a closer match to the requirements for these may point you to the best candidate. You may also feel that one candidate is a better team fit than the other, even though their scores are identical.

Key idea: Ensure fairness

Make the interview as fair as possible to avoid any legal challenge at a later date. Your decision must be based on facts and demonstrate a good and fair process of selection.

Appraisal decisions

Before starting this section, try the activity below.

Undertaking the appraisal of another staff member can incur a number of decisions that need to be made. For example, you will have to form a view on the quality of their work, their attitude, the successes they have achieved and any targets not met. There may be disagreement between the two of you, or there may even be a performance issue (such as poor timekeeping) that you need to address. All of this may end in a decision regarding their work and perhaps a pay award. No wonder the situation can feel loaded with concern, but this need not be the case.

There are three issues here where you need to maintain focus:

▶ **Fairness**
As with recruitment, you must be fair. That means no favouritism, no giving or withholding work projects or training programmes that are not available to everyone. Deal with everyone as if they were on a level platform.

▶ **Being factual**
You cannot make a vague statement such as, 'Someone told me that you are often in late.' This is hearsay, and would be laughed out of court in any legal challenge over fairness. If you are dealing with performance issues, you must deal with facts: 'You were 15 minutes late on Wednesday and 20 minutes late on Friday. Can you explain why this was so?'

▶ **Having a robust process**
Most organizations that hold annual appraisals will provide guidance notes that explain the process to everyone involved. If your organization does this, make sure you follow the system or process suggested. The aim of having a structure to the process is not to

restrict you but to add a professional robustness to the procedure, should there be any queries later on.

The final point is that the appraisal process should not contain any surprises. What that means is if there is a performance problem, you should be dealing with that immediately and not leaving it until the appraisal. Similarly, if good performance is regular, then good feedback should also be given regularly. Managing staff as an ongoing process should prevent you having to make big decisions or have confrontations at appraisal time.

Developing others to make decisions

One of the prime roles of a manager should be developing others. It is essential to develop staff so that they have interesting and challenging work and can be developed to become the managers of the future (this is called succession planning). If staff are developed effectively, it means that they will be able to support you in your work – for example, deputizing for you while you are away.

Some managers may worry about developing staff, fearing that they will then take over their job, but this is irrational. As a manager you will always be one step ahead of any staff member, tackling larger and more complex projects, and be in ultimate control. As a manager you should also be looking at your own development through mentoring or being involved in peer groups such as action learning sets. Developing a staff member or your whole team will give you the time to do this; after all, if you are still making all the smaller decisions you will not have time to take on the larger, more strategic ones, let alone future development for yourself.

Start by taking time to think through the skills that your staff or team already has. Now refer back to the beginning of this book, where we considered the skills required for decision making. How do they match? Are there areas where some learning needs to take place? If so, how could you ensure that your staff member or team is able to acquire that skill?

If you have a human resources or training department, you will be able to ask for their help, but even if your company is not large enough to have its own training officer, there are many programmes on the open market in addition to books and learning aids. Look at the list at the end of this book.

The most important part of skills development is to ensure that the learning is put in the context of the task and embedded back into the business. What this means is explaining to the staff member why they are going on this training programme, and discussing how they can use what they have learned in the context of their decision making.

Remember this: Keep a record of staff training
Don't forget to record your staff development training, so that you can discuss it later in any future appraisal or when you actually delegate part of your work.

Delegating decisions

If you have ensured that your team or staff member is now sufficiently skilled to start decision making in your place, you may want to go a little further and delegate some areas of your work completely. Delegating work should not be:

▶ getting rid of the difficult or boring parts
▶ deliberately making someone's work more difficult
▶ a way of shifting your pile of work on to someone else.

Instead, it should be:

▶ a method of further developing someone
▶ a way of ensuring that your work is covered if you are away
▶ an opportunity for someone to experience being a supervisor or manager.

Remember this: It's still your responsibility
You can delegate the work but not the responsibility. You must support staff and check their delegated tasks to help them to improve and gain confidence. You will find that when you delegate tasks, some people will relish the opportunity to shine while others will worry about making a mistake. What is important is that you strike a balance between trusting staff to work on your behalf and keeping a careful eye on their decisions, to ensure that they meet with your approval.

▶ Knowing the strategy of your organization can help you make decisions relevant to the organization's future.
▶ Operational decisions permeate the fast pace of working life, but you don't have to hurry – take time if you want to.
▶ Involving others in your decision making can help in some circumstances.

▶ The secret in making fast decisions when negotiating lies in the preparation. Even if you don't know the other party you can prepare by thinking about what outcome they would want, and work out some wants and concessions of your own.

▶ Regulate decisions about staff performance by managing them as you go through the year.

Chris has involved his team at the print works but he has not yet thought of delegating any decisions; he thought that was his role. He takes this conundrum to his tutor at the adult education centre. She explains to him that, although there needs to be an authority figure at work, that person does not have to do everything or make every decision. She tells him that when the supervisor trusts others and develops them to do aspects of the supervisor's job, it can free the supervisor up to undertake more challenging projects. She asks Chris to think of three areas of his work that he could delegate to team members. She tells him that they must be projects that they can take over fully and work on, with Chris monitoring only on a daily or weekly basis. Chris realizes that his tutor has been mentoring him and that he may need this type of help later. He notes in his diary for next year that he needs to find a mentor to help his own future development.

Although Pat is a hairdresser, she cannot be in the salon every day if she is also to run the business, and so she needs a deputy. It has to be not only someone she trusts but also someone who will make the best decisions for her business. She observes each team member in action. Jean has been there the longest, but Pat feels that the newest stylist, Sasha, is the best person for the job. She knows her decision will cause problems and so she decides to divide her main work up into four parts and give everyone a task. This way she hopes that no one will be offended. To start with, and in the event of Pat not being there, Jean is to take over Pat's customers, Ben is to look after the finance, Muriel is to be in charge of opening and closing the shop, and Sasha is to deal with any orders, stock and materials. She has also booked time in her diary to revisit this in three months to see how this division of her role is working out.

Next Step

You should now have an idea of the areas where decision making is in operation within a working environment. Delegating decisions can be difficult; after all, when you wanted to be a manager or supervisor it was so that you could shape the business with your knowledge and experience, but you must develop others so that the business can survive while you are away on leave, off sick or at conferences. In the next chapter we will be looking at how emotions can cloud our decisions and what effect this can have on the decision-making process.

8

Decisions clouded by emotions

Goal: To identify when and why your decisions may be affected by emotion and to find a workable solution.

Self-assessment

Read the following statements about emotions and decisions, and say how much you agree with them by circling one of the numbers. If you disagree with the statement circle the 1, if you neither agree nor disagree circle the 3, and if you fully agree circle the 5:

I never feel awkward about my emotions	1 2 3 4 5
I never allow emotions to cloud my decisions	1 2 3 4 5
I can keep my decision processes separate from my emotions	1 2 3 4 5
I rarely cry	1 2 3 4 5
I believe that people who show emotions are weak	1 2 3 4 5
I believe that you can easily distance yourself from emotional decision making	1 2 3 4 5
I dislike being with emotional people	1 2 3 4 5
I believe that people should learn to be more objective	1 2 3 4 5
Work should be separate from home life	1 2 3 4 5
I never have problems making decisions	1 2 3 4 5
Now add up your score and put the total in the box. **Total score =**	

Score	Result
41–50	You do not enjoy working with emotional people or making decisions that others may react to emotionally. Perhaps you cannot understand why people feel the need to be guided by their emotions, and you may feel uncomfortable around those who make decisions by 'gut feeling'. You need to consider that not everyone is the same as yourself and that there are occasions when decisions have to be made at an emotional level rather than a practical one.
26–40	You are fairly confident in your ability to work with the emotions of others or at a personal emotional level. You recognize that there are times when we all make decisions emotionally, but that the best way of ensuring success in these decisions is also (perhaps) to test them at a practical level.
Below 25	You are either a very emotional person or you have an unstructured approach to decision making. Beware: unstructured decision making and making random choices are not the same as making emotional decisions. The former describes a lazy or haphazard attitude, whereas the latter is to do with accessing your intuition. Have a good, long think about which one is you!

We have already looked briefly at the role of emotions in our lives, and how, on some occasions, we make decisions based on other things such as reasoned analysis. Before we are too hard on ourselves, let's remember there may be many reasons why we do this, and that, in some instances, our emotions (or gut feeling) turn out to be correct.

Think about the most recent big decision you had to make – a decision that affected you personally. Did you take a rational approach and complete a matrix? Did you undertake an analysis *before* making the decision? How did it turn out?

What is going on?

Why do we otherwise rational human beings go to pieces when our emotional strings are tweaked? What is the trigger, and what can we do about it? We must first acknowledge that we may not be as in control of our feelings as we think we are.

One of the most powerful human emotions is guilt (particularly for women), and many people exploit this fact to force through their ideas or doctrines. We are exceptionally attuned to guilt, and if we feel bad about something we may act irrationally to trigger a defence mechanism. We employ many defence mechanisms, one of which may be to avoid a difficult situation by running away.

To put that into the context of a decision, imagine that a young man has met a young woman whom he likes very much. She tells him that it is her birthday the next day, and he thinks he will surprise her with some flowers. Unfortunately, he completely forgets and two days go by before he remembers. He now feels guilty, not only for not buying flowers or even ringing, but also for forgetting something so recently told to him and so personal. Rather than make an excuse or apologize, he decides to avoid her in future. The young woman is left wondering what has happened – she thought he liked her.

In that example we see a miscommunication, where the decision to buy flowers becomes the decision to avoid her completely. If you read it through again, I am sure, like me, you will think it sounds irrational – surely the girl would understand if he apologized, and wouldn't that be worth trying rather than losing the promise of a loving relationship? But this is what can happen when emotions become entangled with decisions. The sensible and logical action becomes squeezed out by the emotional guilt, and an opportunity is lost.

What can we do about an emotional situation bearing down on a decision we have to make? Since emotions are stronger than rational thinking (as anyone who has been in love knows), we cannot always stop them. However, we can work with them, see them for what they are, and build our decisions around them. Earlier in the book I mentioned emotional intelligence and how important it is to understand our emotions and work with them. When you know how you tend to react, you can try to find ways around a situation by putting deliberate blocking or minimizing mechanisms in place. For example, if you already know or like (at a personal level) one of the applicants attending an interview, you can decide to ask a colleague to sit in on the interview with you, to reduce bias.

Remember this: Emotions can be useful

Understanding how we operate and bring our emotions into the conscious area of the brain can enable us to put in place deliberate mechanisms that will help us cope with a situation more effectively.

Dealing with family decisions

Dealing with decisions within the family can cause all manner of problems, mainly due to the covert web of private agendas. At work you may have a 'shoot from the hip' attitude and feel able to deal with the consequences of tough talk, but things may be very different at home. Most people's welfare hinges on a number of key relationships that are driven by emotional attachments such as love, nurture and even rivalry and jealousy. We may refrain from speaking quite so directly to the person who provides us with food, clean laundry, a comfortable home and so forth. These complex relationships mean that you may think twice before upsetting family members, and that is why we often hear of forthright people at work behaving very differently at home.

A family also has a number of hidden codes that it abides by. These codes are most noticeable when you meet a new partner and you are expected to share a family ritual such as Christmas. Each family has its own unique way of 'doing Christmas', and this can often be quite confusing to the other party.

Think about how many hidden codes you can spot in your family. Start by completing the sentence, 'In our family we always…' It can be anything, from everyone taking their shoes off as soon as they come indoors to dinner always being served at 6.30.

All these codes are linked to the shared emotions we have, and they ultimately refine our decisions. For example, while you might have no problem telling your manager that you will not be able to come in over the holiday period, you may quake at the thought of telling your family that you will not be able to attend its traditional Boxing Day turkey curry party. The worst thing that can happen at work is that you lose your job, and in any case workplace arguments usually blow over quickly. However, family arguments can escalate and then fester for years, causing deep psychological damage and unhappiness.

Where possible, it is best to work within the family structure and be realistic regarding the consequences of stepping outside it. If decisions you have made upset the balance, try to keep the lines of communication open if at all possible. Once there is a rift in the family, it can become ingrained and make the situation ten times more difficult to repair.

Key idea: Families are complex

Families are unique in their structure. You don't always have to give in to family pressure, but be aware of the consequences of upsetting your family members as a result of your decisions. Families often provide a web of support you may not be aware of.

Decisions with children

Emotional decisions with children are also a very complex dynamic. Complicating the decision this time is that you want to assert your role as an adult but also be supportive and a role model for their future. This makes even a simple decision such as 'Can we eat at

the burger bar?' turn into a decision nightmare, as you think to
yourself:

- The burger bar is not really healthy food – so no.
- On the other hand, they have been good lately and deserve a
  treat – so yes.
- They'll think I am a pushover if I agree – so no.
- Perhaps they will like me more and be better behaved if I agree –
  so yes.
- They might respect me more if I stick to my principles – so no.

Suddenly, what should have been a quick decision has become a
problem that has taken hold of you, and you feel that whatever
you ultimately decide will speak volumes about you, your style of
parenting and the impact on the future of mankind!

Giving in may seem like an easy option this time, but you will find
that suddenly two burger meals a week becomes the new rule as you
have now set a precedent. Next time you say no, your children will
reply 'Well, we did it last week,' leaving you with yet more explaining
to do. It is time to get a grip and take a step backwards, and at the
same time get things in perspective.

Children will ask you to make decisions, seemingly with ideas off
the top of their head. The first lesson here is to question them about
where their thought came from. It may be that they just heard their
friend mention the burger bar and they were echoing somebody else's
desire rather than their own.

Here are some guidelines for making decisions with children:

- **Listen to them carefully**
It is always tempting to say no to children before they have really
explained themselves.

- **Offer children choices**
For example, say, 'You can have your bath now or in half an hour.
You can decide.' This gives children an opportunity to begin to make
decisions for themselves, and offers them a feeling of control.

- **Have rules and boundaries**
For example, if you allow your children one burger meal a week,
stick to that rule. If you need to explain to them that they have
already had that meal, give your reasons for the rule. Boundaries

are really important for children to feel safe, but don't make the rules too complicated. Everyone needs to know the system and how it works.

▶ **Put your rules and boundaries into action**

Believe it or not, many people fall at this final hurdle. They instigate star charts, naughty corners and a whole manner of other boundaries, only to fail to implement them either because they are too busy or it is inconvenient at the time.

Key idea: Model the way

> You may not be aware of it, but as an adult you are teaching children how to make decisions based on your own way of doing this. As in all aspects of life, your children are looking to you as their role model for how they should behave in the future.

The expectancy effect

This is a psychological phenomenon that occurs when decisions are being taken at an emotional level. Basically it can be explained as your brain working in overdrive and creating an image and sometimes even a backstory, before you have even been introduced to someone or found out about something.

It can be better explained through an example, and so let's say that you have two candidates coming to see you for a job. Both look good on paper but the first is Carla Taylor-Smythe who gives an address in a fashionable part of town. The other is Hilda Biggins who appears to live on a somewhat troublesome estate that you have read about in the newspapers. By now you are probably already getting an idea of the people and what they look like, and possibly also imagining their lives. It is not difficult to get carried away, and the connections that your mind is making are exactly the ones that authors expect their readers to make – that is why creating the right name and place is so important in novels. In other words, we are in danger, before we even meet these characters, of expecting them to be certain people and possibly even being biased towards one of them.

The expectancy effect can be a real problem in interviews and it is for this reason that many organizations remove the name and address from the initial sifting information. It would be just too easy to slip into the trap of making a decision on false information, before the person has even set foot in the room.

Stereotyping

When we stereotype people we automatically limit them, so that to our mind they exemplify all that the stereotype represents. You may have heard someone say something like, 'He has a tattoo [or earring, hoodie, unusual hairstyle] and I know all about that type of person.' When people say such things they are assuming that the person bears all the personality and attitudes of that stereotype.

Stereotypes are very common in our culture, and we see them every night on television. Every soap opera and comedy show has its stereotypical single mother, mother-in-law, bully, farmhand and so forth. If stereotypes did not exist, we would not laugh at these characters and their antics because we would not recognize them. It is their familiarity that draws us into the joke and allows us to anticipate their actions – but TV characters are not real. Human beings are far more complex than can be represented in a TV play.

However, we need to be aware of the deeper aspects of stereotyping that may cloud our decisions. The stereotypes we recognize are often the result of our own early experiences or they come from comments made by parents or significant adults when we were young. They lie dormant in the brain and then can pop up unexpectedly. For example, you may be at a party and be introduced to someone new, and take an instant like or dislike to them. If you have ever experienced this, it is your stereotype framework at work. Something about the person has triggered a long forgotten memory upon which you have created a stereotype. The problem is that it is the stereotype that you are now reacting to – not the real person.

We make an amazing number of social decisions in this way. We choose whether to talk to someone, ask them on a date or try to be friends with them without knowing anything about them or having spoken to them. This is demonstrated effectively at family weddings. Weddings are unique in that you have been invited to share a celebration although you probably don't know at least half of the other guests. There is no need for you all to get along because the occasion lasts only a few hours. You will see people form small cliques with people they know, and there will be much pointing and guessing about who is who in the other family, together with the making of wild assumptions: 'That must be her Auntie Linda, you know, the one that ran off with the window cleaner. I could tell it was her.'

To get away from stereotyping people, we need to bring our stereotypes into the open and acknowledge them. Then we can see them for what they are and even question their validity. Go and speak to the guy with the tattoos or the girl with the Mohican hairstyle, and then make up your own mind based on your experience of them as a person, rather than assuming the stereotype.

Try it now

Think of some physical characteristic of people that makes you feel uncomfortable, such as a beard, a large nose or curly hair. Ask yourself why that may be – is it really rational? Does it mean that everyone with that characteristic is the same? Can you decide to ignore that characteristic?

Halo and horns

The halo or horns effect is a combination of stereotyping and expectation put into practice. We are drawn to some people and find others difficult to like – and this can be a very individual thing. Someone that you feel drawn to may be the same person that sends others running for the hills.

The problem with this is when this starts to cloud our behaviour and consequently our decision making. When you automatically like someone or feel drawn to them (the halo effect), in your eyes they can do no wrong. You may forgive them anything, or offer them privileges that you would not offer others (this happens at work and in your home life). Conversely, when you automatically take a dislike to someone (the horns effect), you may find fault with everything they do and even withhold privileges.

You may see this in the office setting when managers send their favourite people on expensive training programmes while not allowing those they dislike to go. You also see it in families and social circles.

Again, the secret of ensuring that you don't fall into this trap is to be very aware of your own feelings towards others, and to question whether your feelings are rational and your actions justifiable. Using the above example of training courses, you should be sending the most appropriate person who needs and will use the information, irrespective of your feelings towards them.

Negative bias

Sometimes we can know too much about others, and that can then affect our emotions and the way in which we make decisions about them. You may be prejudiced towards someone before you have even met them, often because of hearsay or gossip, and this is called negative bias.

Everyone has a past, and most people would say that in life they have not always been perfect; after all, that is what learning is all about. Without the mistakes and low periods of our life, we cannot develop our skills so that we perform better in future. However, the past is just that – the past – and everyone deserves to be assessed on their current actions and behaviour rather than some unreliable story of old.

Let me give you an example of negative bias in action. You have arranged to meet a new business contact at an event. You do not know this person but you have heard that they are very successful and so you are really keen to work with them. While you are waiting, you bump into another friend and explain why you are there. You tell them that you have not met this contact but that she will be wearing a blue suit with a white shirt. Your friend looks uncomfortable and tells you that she has just seen someone of that description going through the pockets of coats in the cloakroom, clearly looking for wallets and purses. How do you feel about working with that person now? Even though the information was somewhat questionable, it has sown the seed of doubt in your mind.

Five minutes later your contact arrives, and suddenly you feel less at ease; you find yourself clutching your bag tightly and refuse when she offers to take your coat – and even when your friend rushes up to you later and tells you that the person she saw you with was not the same one as in the cloakroom, you still feel uneasy. Suddenly you are not as confident about working with this person and your mind goes into overdrive: is that how they made their money? Perhaps they are not that successful at all. You are now firmly in the grip of negative bias and it is only when you see it for what it is that you will be able to break free.

The phenomenon of negative bias explains why it is so difficult for people who have worked in a troublesome team or been labelled troublemakers to be redeployed to a new team. They may have had nothing to do with the situation and be no more troublesome than any other member of staff, but the negativity surrounding their situation creates expectations and assumptions that drive your behaviour towards them. If you are suspicious and lack trust in their abilities, their reaction may be to challenge you, a move that seems to confirm that they are 'difficult' to manage, and the label becomes a self-fulfilling prophecy.

It is for this reason that it is sometimes better not to know any background information about a person or a problem, so that the decisions you make can be based on your own first-hand information rather than a mix of misinformation and other people's ideas.

> **Remember this: Not all reputations are deserved**
> People do make mistakes but they may also be victims of negative bias, so it's important to give everyone a chance by making your own decisions about them in the fullness of time rather than jumping to conclusions based on third-party evidence.

Power differences

When looking at emotional reactions to decision making, we also need to consider power differences. We are all aware of the power differences around us, even if this is at a subliminal level.

Power need not be based on roles and hierarchical relationships, such as that between managers and their staff. Power can also be:

▶ bestowed by others (perhaps looking up to someone as a leader)
▶ related to money and possessions (those with a big house or an expensive car)
▶ related to talent or expertise (a top footballer or musician)

- ▶ linked to a powerful status or title (a famous actor or maybe a lord or dame)
- ▶ linked to charisma or personality (some people simply have presence and everyone notices when they walk into a room).

However, it is the effect of that power that we need to consider. When power is not evenly in balance it can cause distortions in decision making. If someone appears more powerful to us, we may feel automatically compromised in our objective decision making and there is a danger that we will just agree with them. (For example, if you have ever met a film star or other celebrity you may have been struck dumb just by being near them. You are effectively unable to function!)

Link that power difference with any of the other issues we have mentioned above, such as the halo effect, and it becomes highly likely that we are not reacting objectively. Many powerful, good-looking bosses marvel at how easy it is, sometimes, to push through difficult changes. Perhaps it is not their skill in leadership that has made this happen, but something to do with the power they hold and the halo effect. This can be a good thing when the change is the right one, but many CEOs have made a poor decision and still everyone has followed them, believing in their vision of the future even though, in retrospect, they have claimed to know it was flawed.

Key idea: Power differences can work both ways

Power can be associated with great leadership, but there is also the possibility of ascribing power to someone who cannot deliver. If you are in a negotiating relationship, it helps if both parties are equal in the power they exert to negate any direct influence.

- ▶ Emotions can impinge on our rational decision making but not always negatively.
- ▶ Try to acknowledge and work with the issues that family members or children bring to the decision-making process.
- ▶ Be aware of certain psychological phenomena that surround making decisions about and around people.
- ▶ Challenge any stereotypes and make your own decisions about people.
- ▶ Be aware of how power can affect us emotionally and distort our decisions.

Chris has settled into his job. He knows he has a lot to learn but he is starting to feel more at ease with his role as supervisor and running a team. However, his new-found confidence is shaken when he is accused of favouritism by one of his staff members. Chris has allowed a team member, Steve, to research a new technique. Steve is also a good friend and, even though he was the best person for the task, Chris realizes that he probably acted emotionally in asking him. He also fell into the trap of not discussing the decision with everyone, mainly because of time constraints. He now has to find a way through this problem and rebuild the team's trust. He wishes now that he had thought this through beforehand, but he also knows that, as a new supervisor, he will make these mistakes and he can take this learning into the future.

Pat also has a problem that concerns personalities and past history. Under the salon's previous owner Pat was considered the main stylist, but now that she will own the salon and run the business she does not want to do so much frontline styling. Everyone is now vying to be named the main stylist. Jean has been there the longest and is the most experienced (although most of her customers want older styles), Ben is the most creative but only works there three days a week and Sasha specializes in dyes and colouring hair. There is also the problem that Pat has had several arguments with Jean in the past. Pat recognizes that the decision cannot be made emotionally or with gut feelings because, in a small team, a wrong decision could tear them apart and she does not want to lose anyone. She therefore decides not to have a head stylist but three specialists, each with their own area of expertise. To make this clear to the customers, Pat puts up a sign announcing the new specialists. This decision also has the benefit that no one has a pay increase, elevating them above the others.

Next Step

It is essential to consider whether our decision making is emotional or rational: there are risks attached to each approach. No one chooses a life partner based on a spreadsheet calculation but, equally, a business decision based on gut feelings would be difficult to justify. The following chapter looks at techniques to help us make better life-changing decisions.

9

Life-changing decisions

Goal: To consider the larger decisions in our life – ones that literally can change our lives – and how we should be making those decisions.

Read the following statements about life-changing decisions, and say how much you agree with them by circling one of the numbers. If you disagree with a statement circle the 1, if you neither agree nor disagree circle the 3, and if you fully agree circle the 5:

I am clear about my future and where I want to be	1 2 3 4 5
I am comfortable with making decisions about my future	1 2 3 4 5
I don't mind when life throws up surprises	1 2 3 4 5
I like to be in total control of my life	1 2 3 4 5
My friends would not describe me as a relaxed person	1 2 3 4 5
I believe the life I want is out there and I just need to go and grab it	1 2 3 4 5
I love change	1 2 3 4 5
I have been known to take risks with my career	1 2 3 4 5
I am always thinking ahead and attempting to plan my life	1 2 3 4 5
I believe that all change offers opportunity	1 2 3 4 5
Now add up your score and put the total in the box. **Total score =**	

Score	Result
41–50	You certainly feel comfortable with change and you may even instigate changes in your life without them happening naturally. You are confident and strong and have a good sense of where you are going in life. However, you might like to consider whether you may be a little too rigid in your quest. Having a strong focus is one thing but becoming fixated or obsessed to the exclusion of all other ideas is quite another. Your strong level of focus probably makes it easy for you to make the decision, but consider the other options, too.
26–40	You are fairly confident in your ability to deal with change and the large decisions that crop up in life. You accept that these decisions occur periodically in our lives and that you need to consider all options before making your decision. You are pragmatic and, although you feel able to make these decisions (and live with the consequences), a little more confidence is always good.
Below 25	You feel uncomfortable with change, and having to make decisions in your life makes you feel vulnerable. Perhaps you realize early on that your response will be life changing, and that scares you. You may even be prone to freeze and do nothing, like a rabbit caught in the headlights. Alternatively, you may feel so relaxed that you let life's problems wash over you, and allow events to take their own course naturally.

Every so often, life throws up situations when some key decisions have to be made. They are key decisions because they can alter the course of our lives.

When was the last time you made a key decision that affected your life, and what was it? How did you make that decision? When do you hope to know, or how do you know, whether the decision was a good one?

We are often not consistent in the way we make many of our larger life decisions. For example, it is astonishing that many people spend more time on deciding which car to buy than they do on deciding which house to buy, even though the house will cost many times more and will possibly be the most expensive thing they will ever buy. Most people visit a house they are thinking of buying only once or twice, while a car purchase may merit several viewings and test drives. The same is true of a holiday destination. We often research the location avidly, even though the holiday is only for one or two weeks. We usually spend much less time researching a company to work for, even though we will have to live with that decision for far longer. We need to recognize these life-changing decisions for what they are and consider whether a little more effort in making such decisions could result in more satisfying outcomes.

Remember this: Some decisions are always hard

This chapter covers a range of life decisions that you may find difficult from a personal perspective. If you have trouble accepting even the most logical approach to your actions, please seek counselling advice. There may be some deep reason for your anxiety and guilt that would benefit from some discussion.

Serendipity, chance or a great decision?

I believe that chance and opportunity come to everyone equally, but that people who see and grab opportunities are the ones who can really make things happen. I am sure you have heard people say such things as, 'It's strange how I came to be here. A friend of a friend offered me a ticket and I was unsure, but decided to come, and that is where I met…' In other words, it sounds like serendipity. While some of this is about chance, there is also the all-important fact that the person took the decision to go to the event where they subsequently met someone significant. Whether they were going to complete that sentence by saying that they met the love of their lives, a celebrity or the person who would offer them a great career opportunity, it is clear that they took the opportunity while someone else might have stayed at home.

Let me give you a further example. Years ago I used to be in a job that required me to go to a great number of meetings. I was always being told, 'Meetings are so boring. You never learn anything and have to sit through a load of —.' You get the gist. However, I discovered that if you go into every meeting thinking that it will be boring, that is exactly what it will be. I decided, instead, to go into every meeting with a 'What will I learn today?' attitude and constantly look for opportunities within the content of the meeting that would be of interest to me or benefit my team. By doing this I was able not only to sit through meetings without becoming bored and negative, but also to spot opportunities that passed others by. I would come out of every meeting with four or five action points, useful information or good ideas to pass on to my team. Was I some kind of magician? No, the same information was there for everyone, but I took the decision to do something with it.

THE SENSITIZED BRAIN

I found opportunities because I was looking for opportunities. I could do this because the brain is very good at looking for things when it knows what it is searching for. We all subliminally take in thousands of images every day from advertising, the TV, posters and magazines. The brain can handle this enormous amount of data but we cannot, and so we have filters built into our brain that allow us to select or highlight important facts or recognize data and images that are important to us.

Imagine you wanted to buy a red car. Suddenly you will see red cars everywhere, in advertisements, on TV and on the road – it is as if there are more red cars about than any other colour. This process is called sensitization. When the brain is sensitized, it is looking for that particular thing, and seeks to find it (a bit like a search engine on a computer). We often think that situations are luck, when in fact it is our sensitized brain that is working overtime, trying to find matches, links and solutions to help you.

> **Key idea: Anyone can sensitize their brain**
>
> Anyone can sensitize their brain to filter opportunities.
> Sometimes you make your own chances in life; it is said that
> luck is 1 per cent inspiration and 99 per cent perspiration. Go
> looking for opportunities and you will find them.

Now, let's look at some of the major decisions you may need to make
in life and the aspects you need to consider.

Choosing (or losing) a partner

This is another area of your life where you are in a legal scenario
and yet acting emotionally. This is because, when you marry,
form a partnership, or progress a relationship to a more formal
situation (such as living together), your actions, however emotional,
become subject to the law. At a time when you are highly charged
emotionally, the law is being applied coldly. As we have discussed
previously, this can be a difficult combination. Beneath the emotional
commitment lies a binding contract that requires you to form a legal
partnership with another person.

Yet, some people are only too ready to sign this contract before even
considering whether they are compatible with the other person. How
do they feel about children? What about the rest of the family; does
this person fit in? How will we divide our income? In no other area
of your life would you sign a contract without asking important
practical questions (even when buying a vacuum cleaner you would
find out the length of the guarantee), and yet you may be feeling that
these questions seem *unromantic*. Unfortunately, romance often
seems to fade somewhat abruptly anyway, and when marriages and
partnerships break up some of the most common reasons cited are:

▶ one partner wants children and the other does not
▶ the family does not like him or her
▶ finances, and who pays for what.

Although we don't want to reduce our relationship completely to a
spreadsheet exercise, it can still be helpful to consider listing *fors* and
againsts, together with a stakeholder analysis, both for now and how
you perceive the situation will be in years to come. The timeframe
example is particularly useful because another issue here is that

emotional thinking tends to be in the present moment. You might feel very different the following day or even in a year's time. As the saying goes, 'Act in haste, repent at leisure', and that is exactly what many of us do. Projecting your thoughts into the future and taking time to consider what you could gain and what you could lose can therefore be a useful exercise.

> **Remember this: We all change throughout our lives**
> Someone we think of as dull when we are in our 20s we may describe as solid and dependable in our 40s. Conversely, someone we consider wacky and original in our 30s may be an embarrassment to us when we are in our 60s.

Selecting a school or university

Education is incredibly important, but it is not just about the learning itself: the environment in which the learner is placed also helps to determine their success. Therefore it is not sufficient just to send your child to the best school educationally; it must also be about 'personal fit'. Naturally, you would consider distance and practicality in addition to grades and the school report, but here are some additional key questions that may help you decide on the right school for your child:

▶ **Is your child extrovert or introvert?**
It can help to know this because if the school values outward shows of confidence and your child is introverted or reflective in nature, this may not be the best fit.

▶ **What does the curriculum include?**
Some schools do not cover Shakespeare, teach an additional language or study music in depth. Whether or not this is important will depend on your child's skills, aptitudes and future hopes. Some schools now offer a completely alternative curriculum alongside the standard one.

▶ **What is the reward structure and how are pupils motivated?**
Most workplaces offer staff rewards for when they do well. This is usually in the form of a bonus, pay rise or gift of some kind. Motivation can be learned early and therefore it is important that you find out how the school rewards pupil achievement.

▶ **Is each child seen as an individual?**
Every child develops at his/her own rate and this needs to be reflected in the way they are encouraged and any targets they are asked to

achieve. If your child is a late learner, a highly competitive classroom atmosphere may cause unnecessary anxiety.

For university you will also need to consider the following:

▶ **Distance from home**

If the student finds it difficult to settle or has hobbies at home that they want to maintain, you need to be realistic about how many times you are prepared to help with transport (in time and cost) to and from university.

▶ **The environment**

Some students love to work in new and modern environments, while others may prefer a more traditional setting.

▶ **The ranking**

All universities have reputations and are ranked in league tables. This may or may not matter to you but it might be important to future employers (especially blue-chip companies), who will often give preference to those who studied in one of the top universities for their subject.

▶ **The course**

Not all courses are the same and it is essential that the programme of study include areas of interest, strength and development. For example, some students might want a high level of coursework rather than mostly exams.

Key idea: The student needs to be content

> Think curriculum content, atmosphere, environment and location, and agree this with the student involved. The decision must suit everyone's needs to be successful and, for effective learning, the student needs to be happy with the decision.

Where to live?

Moving home and deciding where to live seem to be general problems of life that most of us experience at some point. The actual fact of moving is further complicated by other issues such as family ties to an area (such as children already settled in schools or friends in the area), the property ladder (aren't we supposed to make a profit on our property, and aren't we supposed to move progressively to a bigger property?), and property prices (I want and need to live there, but can't afford it). It is so difficult to decide what to do.

Your decision about where to live can cause problems when:

- ▶ your work is elsewhere
- ▶ your family has disparate needs
- ▶ you cannot afford to live where you want to
- ▶ you need to be in a school catchment area.

YOUR WORK IS ELSEWHERE

Perhaps your company has moved or you have changed jobs. You may have decided to sell up and relocate, with the risk of finding that you don't like your new job and that you wish you were back 'home'. You may think that you have to move, but this is not always the case; you can try dipping your toe in the water first.

One way to do this would be to rent out your present home for a few months and then rent another nearer your new place of work. This would give you the benefit of being able to try the new job out for a time while covering the cost of renting with the rent from your property. It would also enable you to get to know the new town and find out about the specific areas or roads that you would be interested in living in. Another key factor may be the daily transport needs that come with your job. The cost of travel is increasing steadily and therefore you need to factor in how far from your place of work you will live, the transport routes and prices, and parking.

YOUR FAMILY HAS DISPARATE NEEDS

There can be divisions between your needs and your children's or between your needs and those of your parents. All family members need our support at key times in their lives and so where we live may be dictated by their needs as much as our own. You may have to find living accommodation within easy reach of your family, but this is not always possible, especially if you have multiple divisions in your family, or family members spread far and wide.

The first point is to acknowledge in yourself that this is not going to be easy, but that you need to find a compromise rather than flounder around. If you can call a family meeting to discuss the issue, do so, but if not then you need to make a decision based on some key criteria such as access, alternative options of care and so forth. The decision needs to be approached systematically and reviewed regularly.

YOU CANNOT AFFORD TO LIVE WHERE YOU WANT TO

Many of us have this dilemma. House prices are based on a range of criteria such as condition, size/space and location. You will need to compromise on one or more of these if you cannot afford them all. If location is the most important factor, perhaps you could consider a renovation project, or be prepared to compromise on size.

Your choice between these two options will depend on an honest appraisal of your skills and the size of your family (and any future plans). Bear in mind that, if you select a desirable home, one that will easily sell again, you can always relocate at a later time or when your situation alters.

YOU NEED TO BE IN A SCHOOL CATCHMENT AREA

The concept of catchment areas comes in and out of fashion, but many parents consider local schools when deciding where to live. Entry into a good school can add a premium to the price of a property and so you may find that you need to spend more to secure this attraction. Conversely, if you don't have children of school age you may decide to avoid these areas, because you are paying for something you will not use. Be aware also that a school's reputation is not always up to date. Go online and locate the government report for each school in the area (www.directgov.gov.uk), and compare them. You may find that a school with a good reputation from the past is now no better than any other, or that other schools have improved their performance recently.

Remember this: Your home need not be for ever

Whatever stage you are at in life, the place where you have decided to live need not be permanent. Unless you are putting down some serious roots, houses can always be sold and you can move to another area in the fullness of time. However, you need to acknowledge that not everyone in the family finds relocating easy, so consider their needs, too.

Changing work or career

Years ago the concept of changing your work or career was dramatic. Now it is almost commonplace. Life is a cycle and staying nimble in your career is essential, as technological advances have made many careers and jobs for life obsolete. The good news is that advances in personal development mean that we can now retrain for almost any career and change career several times in our lifetime.

Whether you want to change your place of work or your entire career, unless you live alone, your decision is likely to have an impact on other people. Therefore you need to consider:

▶ whether this means moving to another part of the country or even abroad (there could be implications for schools and family)

▶ the financial implications of returning to home study (and how that affects others)

▶ whether there is a future in your new career (for example, we will always need builders and plumbers but the number of estate agents has reduced dramatically in recent years)

▶ the amount of passion you have for your new chosen career (because, when times are difficult, you will need that passion to maintain motivation)

▶ whether you have sufficient information about your new career or place of work (two days of research could prevent two years of suffering if you realize that you have made a mistake)

▶ who will help you in your quest (it is great if someone supports you and tough if they don't)

▶ whether this is really the best time to be doing this (either in the year, or in your life).

Remember this: Realism is vital

Changing your job or your career can be liberating and bring a whole new uplift to your life, but be realistic. For example, if you are in your 40s and want to retrain to be a nurse, you need to recognize that it is a very physical job and you may not have as much energy as someone in their 20s. You also need to acknowledge that the training will take several years and that returning to study can be a challenge if you have not maintained the academic side of your development.

Deciding when relatives need care

One of the most difficult decisions you may need to take in your adult life is that of handing over the care of a much-loved parent or relative to someone else. We might think that we will never be in this situation, but it is increasingly likely to happen because we are all living longer than ever before. Elderly care has become one of the fastest-growing industries as increased life expectancy, together with more people living away from family for work, has resulted in a situation where we are not able to care for our elderly relatives simply because we no longer live nearby.

When you make this decision it is essential that you consider what is best for the relative in question. Placing them at the very centre of your decision will ensure that you make the best possible decision for them. To feel justified in your decision you need to know that this outcome offers them the best that life can provide in their later years.

However difficult the decision is, it is imperative that you are able to look yourself in the mirror and assert that, even in the most difficult of circumstances, you made the best selection that was possible for them.

Deciding to start a family

There is a truth in the old adage that if you tried to justify the reasons to start a family you never would, because it is too expensive and takes too much time – but where would the human race be then? It is good that so many of us choose to ignore that advice and instead decide to add to our numbers – but when to do it? That is the big decision!

Basically youth and good health are on our side when we have children young, but career, confidence and finance can seem more favourable when we are older. Age also plays a role, particularly with women, as fertility drops as age increases. Added to this mix is the fact that many people now have second and even third families as relationships move on and people have more than one partner during their lifetime.

No one can really tell you when is the right time to start a family, and if you asked five people they would probably all give you different answers based on their own experience. If you and your partner feel ready, don't allow any naysayers to interrupt your plans. For many people, any negative aspects of having a family are usually cancelled out by the change in their value system once their little ones appear. Ask any parent how they manage and I expect they will tell you that they don't know – they just do.

Deciding to take a career break

Taking a career break can happen at any time, but the reason for it is likely to vary according to your stage in life:

- Taken early in your career, it usually signifies unrest and wanting to either travel or try out another career for a time.
- Taken later on in your career, it tends to indicate that you feel established and able to take some time out for adventure, or perhaps you feel that your youth is passing you by.

Whatever your reasoning, you need to accept that not every employer looks favourably on career breaks. This is because:

- they can be difficult to organize, especially if your expertise is needed regularly
- they can look odd on a CV, and future employers will question why you did this
- they are still viewed as decadent by some employers, who cannot see their value (even a worthy project)
- there is a fear that a career break makes you more 'fly by night' and less committed to the company – not good in times of recession.

Unless your company offers formal career breaks, you will need to sell the benefits to the boss. A career break is not a right; it is a request and as such can be refused. However, if your employer is willing, a career break is a great way of experiencing something new and refreshing your batteries. Once you have the go-ahead, you will need to:

- make sure you have a plan for how your job will be covered while you are away and how it would work when you come back
- ensure that your career break has a focus and some real learning outcomes that ideally link back to your job
- demonstrate how you will stay up to date in your career while you are away
- plan and organize everything before the career break begins (one year goes very fast and if you have to spend the first month organizing everything, that is time wasted when you are not being paid)
- save up some money to tide you over and pay for your break
- make sure everyone knows what you are doing, why you are doing it and how they can stay in touch.

If your employer is willing and the cause is a worthy one, try to secure some local press interest for your trip, which will also show your employer in a good light. However, not all career breaks are for career reasons or travel. You may also request a career break to care for a relative or assist in a family matter.

If you could take a career break, what would you do? How could your activity add to your professional life? What could you discover about yourself?

Deciding the rest of your life

Many people experience a pinchpoint in their lives where they look back over the years and reflect on what they have achieved, and forward into the future when they are reminded that there is not much time to achieve their goals. For many it is already too late to play for England or make the Olympics!

We all have dreams as well as goals. We also know where we should be at certain points in our lives, and these reflective thoughts tend to coincide with birthdays ending in a 0 or a 5. What are you going to do with the rest of your life? Is there any way you can start to make those dreams come true?

It is true that we may not make all of our goals but is there a way of deciding to tap into part of those goals? For example, we may not play for England but we could get involved in a local youth football team. We may not make the Olympics but we could retrain as a sports physiotherapist or sports coach. There are so many ways of developing skills that allow you to tap into the world of your dreams while recognizing your limitations. Life is for living and so, if you feel unfulfilled in one area of your life, decide to do something about it.

It is difficult to think about the future, especially when your nose is to the grindstone, but it's important to consider where you are going in life and whether that journey is still relevant. What do you want to do for the rest of your life? How will you decide what the future offers you?

▶ The decision has to be either yours or a joint one; they cannot be delegated. These are key decisions in your life and you need to have ownership.

▶ Opportunities are there for those who go looking – so set your mind to start looking.

▶ Remember to assess the risks and to include all stakeholders. Many of these decisions concern not only yourself but also family and friends.

▶ Do your homework, be honest, and be bold – and go for it.

▶ Draw a timeline and plan a route towards your success.

Chris has a big decision to make. While on his supervisors' programme he has been noticed by another employer. Print Right is a large national printing company and Douglas, one of its managers, is on the course with Chris. Douglas has heard Chris speak about how he has handled problems at work and has recommended him to his management. They have now approached Chris with a job offer. Chris is amazed; he has never been headhunted before and the offer is a good one. He does not know what to do. Chris draws up criteria to compare the job at Print Right with his own and finds that although the pay appears to be more, he would be in a printing works ten miles away. He would have to buy a car, and would be expected to keep to shop hours including working weekends (which he does not do at the moment). Now this does not seem such a good offer, and he decides to decline. Although it has been a great morale booster, it has also encouraged him to grow the business at Peters & Sons and make his own career work.

Just when things seem organized for Pat, she receives some devastating news: her mother has had a fall and needs her support. Her mother lives five miles away and it is going to be difficult for Pat to continue as a stylist in the business. She needs to make some decisions fast. To start with, she calls her staff together to explain the situation and that things may change over time because she is unsure how her mother will be affected in the long term. She is surprised to find that the team is hugely supportive: Jean has gone through the same situation with her father and Sasha's family is currently looking after her grandmother at home. Pat feels better for explaining everything and even more determined to make everything work, and so she starts to plan a way forward by holding a meeting with all her family members, to discuss how they can all support her mother.

Next Step

This chapter introduced a range of life-changing decisions that we often have to make. No one can make these decisions for us, and all will have distinct effects on our life, whatever we decide. In the following chapter we will consider the decisions we make that carry on beyond our lives and perhaps affect the way we are remembered.

10

Beyond the decisions

Goal: To acknowledge that others may have to live with the decisions we made, recognize the impact this may have, and minimize disruption for others after we have gone.

Self-assessment

Read the following statements about decisions that might affect others after we die, and say how much you agree with them by circling one of the numbers. If you disagree with a statement circle the 1, if you neither agree nor disagree circle the 3, and if you fully agree circle the 5:

I understand how decisions I make today will come into fruition after I have gone	1 2 3 4 5
I am not bothered about being remembered favourably	1 2 3 4 5
I believe in leaving things to fate	1 2 3 4 5
Thinking about decisions that affect a future I am not part of is a waste of time	1 2 3 4 5
I like to live in the present	1 2 3 4 5
I don't care about what happens to others after I have gone	1 2 3 4 5
I don't want to contribute towards society	1 2 3 4 5
I have nothing to leave that is of interest to anyone else	1 2 3 4 5
I believe that people should remember me for my greatness	1 2 3 4 5

I am not bothered about other people and what they think	1 2 3 4 5
Now add up your score and put the total in the box. **Total score =**	

Score	Result
41–50	You are prone to living in the present and may not consider the future other than to think about your own life and how the future affects you. It may be that you don't quite know the ways in which you can make a real contribution to society as well as to your relatives, friends, colleagues and others. Read through the following sections and see where your actions could make a real difference to someone's life.
26–40	You understand that life does not owe you anything but that we are all part of the larger web of society, and that you have a part in that web. Whether you choose to make a dramatic statement or benefit your family, you need to be aware of the legacies that we all leave throughout our lives. That allocation can start now as you start to think through your life and the decisions you made.
Below 25	You may be too aware of the future and how the decisions you make today will affect it – so much so that you may worry unnecessarily about it all. Yes, we may leave many legacies in our lifetime but many of them are unknown, such as the result of giving some great advice to someone. Try to strike a balance with your life; you have plenty to give and plenty to leave.

No one likes to think about their own mortality, but the truth is that none of us will be around for ever and some of the decisions we make in our lifetime will come into effect after we are gone. These decisions may either tarnish or enhance the view that others have of us. You can spend your entire life knowing someone and then have their memory spoiled by not understanding their last wishes or why they chose to take a particular action. It can be very sad when this happens because it is as if all our memories are spoilt by one often ill-thought-out action.

If you have ever watched the perennially favourite film *It's a Wonderful Life*, you will have understood its message that we can all make a difference, and had any one of us not been born the world would be a different place because of that. We are all important and we all have something to give, whether it is ideas, interactions, love, money or something else.

The tombstone shocker

How would you like to be remembered? Write a list of all the adjectives you would like people to associate with you. How can you make sure people remember you in this way?

A common exercise in coaching is to write out your own eulogy or create a memorial that describes how you would like to be remembered. The notion is that from this end you should work backwards and take the decisions today that will result in you achieving that end. It is a good exercise and really brings home to everyone that life is short and that if we are to be remembered in the way we want to be, we have to think about laying the foundations that will make this happen today.

However, I believe there is a deeper message here, and that is to be careful of the *manner* in which you tie up your affairs because, in the same way that miscommunication can happen between friends (and cause a rift that can last for ever), you can intend one outcome but actually cause another. Let me give you an example.

A kind farmer wanted the best for both his sons and always treated them equally. One stayed to work on the farm and the other built a life for himself in town with an office job. When the farmer died he left all the farmland to be divided equally between both his sons (to show that he loved them equally), and all the machinery and livestock to the son who would remain in farming. This seemed fair. Unfortunately, the son who remained on the farm could not farm efficiently with only half the land and needed to buy back the rest of it to make the farm viable. The son who worked in the town did not need the land but wanted the money from it.

While the obvious solution would have been for the farmer son to buy back the other son's land, he could not afford to pay full price for it. Should the other son have sold it at half its value to help his brother? I am sure you can see the conundrum. The brothers soon fell out over the issue, the last thing that the farmer would have wanted. The father's bequest caused his sons pain and anguish and so, as you can imagine, he was less than fondly remembered by either of them. His desire to let them know that he loved them equally was completely overshadowed by the difficult situation. The gesture, rather than being seen as good fortune, became a problem.

We cannot always know how the future will turn out, but there are certain things we can choose to do that can help when we decide how, and in what way, we would like to be remembered.

Remember this: Not all assets are easily divided

For example, companies cannot be sold off and people have certain rights to stay in property if they live on the premises.

Volunteering

In the latter portion of our lives, and when family commitments are a little easier, some people like to leave a living legacy by volunteering to work on a charitable project. This can be in your own town, in the country or even abroad (with an agency such as Voluntary Services Overseas).

There is always a need for skills, both intellectual and practical, to help communities work together through extreme hardship, and you could make a difference that would continue well beyond your own lifetime and touch the lives of many people.

If you feel inspired, there will always be projects within your own community that you can volunteer for, at any age, and with varying levels of commitment. Maybe you would like to be trained to be a Samaritan, a counsellor or an advisor, or perhaps you would prefer to preserve our heritage for the future? There are many ways in which we can all work together to improve communities and give a little back for everything that has been provided for us.

> **Remember this: Not all legacies are financially based**
> Mentoring a group or helping a project to trade in the open market can change the outlook and prospects for an entire village in the developing world. Mentoring a young person in your own locality can change their prospects for the better and encourage them to achieve things they might not otherwise have done.

The legacy of change and rebirth

You may remember a hit TV show many years ago where Sir John Harvey-Jones was invited into various companies to turn them around. It made compelling viewing and the formula has been copied several times since. Sometimes we need a catalyst like this in order to change, otherwise there is a danger that we will carry on doing what we have always done because we feel safe in our small world, even if our business is slowly dying around us.

You can be that catalyst for change, either in your family or your work. Go back to basics and decide what core values you want to preserve, and how you can change things to make an improvement for the future. Whether this means taking a hard line at work on premises, costs, structure or even the staff, you literally could save your business or organization from going bankrupt. Most businesses today are becoming leaner and investing in technology, but still too many are concentrating on the tasks of the moment and not looking to the future. Could you be the one to introduce changes into your workplace that alter the culture and create a better business future?

Deciding to create a lasting memory

Some people like to create a memorial, remembrance cup or trophy for the future: something solid and lasting, when life seems transient and fleeting. This may be linked to a sport or another field of endeavour and usually bears either the name of the person who set it up or their relative. For example, a writer may wish to leave a legacy in the form of an annual writing competition. This would involve a prize in the form of a cup or trophy, often along with a voucher or gift.

It is perfectly fine to create a memorial for yourself. It does not have to be done by others, and you can do it in your own lifetime; it does not have to happen posthumously. The first thing you need to consider is what you want to donate.

A mobile item might be a prize, cup or trophy. If you want to create a memorial in this way, you will need to make provision for the future by means of some form of ongoing bond that will pay out every year. This will fund the award for the future; even solid silver cups need repairing from time to time. If you are thinking of a large silver cup or trophy this will be expensive, so you may also want to add a sum to the bond to cover insurance of the item against loss, damage and theft. Within your bond you also need to allow for inflation so that any prize of cash or tokens remains realistic in the future.

A solid memorial may range from a simple park bench to a grand gesture such as a new ward in a hospital. These are usually one-off payments and do not usually include ongoing funding for maintenance. It is likely that the park bench would display a plaque bearing a message and that the hospital ward would bear your name.

A legacy of learning and living might be a sponsorship agreement. In this case the legacy is less about a monument or building and more about creating a personal impact on a smaller scale. Whether you would like to sponsor a child in a developing country, pay for someone's education, provide a remote village with water or help a community to set up a fair-trade project, there are many organizations who can help you set out your bequest and help you speak to family and friends about your wishes.

A decision to spend money in this way will mean that the profits that you have made in your lifetime go on to provide opportunities for others less fortunate, and the wonderful thing is that it does not take much money to make a tangible difference to the life of someone else. A decision you make while you are alive can literally save other lives or provide children with an education and therefore with opportunities that they might otherwise not have had.

The same provisos about future funding apply here. For example, if you decide to sponsor a child for their education, you must make sure that there will be sufficient funds available for them to complete that education. You will also need to find out as much about your charitable organization as possible beforehand, to ensure that your money is spent in the way you would wish it to be.

Where there's a will...

It is a difficult decision to make a will; it is hard to acknowledge your own mortality. However, it is vitally important to make a will, even if you change it regularly to reflect your mood, because it is the best chance you have of making sure that your decisions and desires are carried out. It also makes your departure easier for your family to cope with because they will have fewer decisions to make on your behalf.

A simple decision not to make a will could mean that your wishes, large and small, are ignored. For example, if you have a piece of jewellery that a friend has always admired and you wish to acknowledge that you valued the friendship by leaving it to them, this is unlikely to happen unless you record that wish in your will.

If you die without making a will, your next of kin will inherit your estate (after any taxes due are paid). Naturally, this may be challenged in court if another party feels that they were entitled to some of the estate, but then it is for someone else to make a decision, not you, and all parties can feel aggrieved (as in the example of the farmer at the beginning of this chapter).

Wills must also remain as current as possible. Although we cannot envisage every eventuality, we need to be as aware as we can. For example, a father had six children but loved his youngest daughter the most. She was small, weak and picked on by the other children, and seemed to need his protection. The years passed, his wife died and he became very ill. To show his love for his youngest daughter, he drew up a will leaving all his money to his five children and all his shares (which were considerable) to her. He was ill for a year and when he died the other five children (all now grown up and married) inherited a fine amount of cash, but his daughter who inherited the shares received practically nothing. This was because, while he was ill, the companies he had shares in lost money, so that the shares became practically worthless.

Again, one decision made in good faith had an unforeseen result. Possibly he could have prevented this if he had been more open about his bequest. Then, perhaps, his youngest daughter would have looked out for warning signs in the companies before the crash happened. Or maybe he could have also left her some of the money as well as the shares, just in case.

Key idea: Make a will

Make a will and communicate your wishes to those who need to know, so that they can keep an eye on the situation for you.

A last-minute decision to marry

Our latter years can become lonely if we live alone. For comfort and companionship, as well as for love, some people decide to marry in their twilight years. However, this happy occasion is sometimes marred by the suspicions of relatives who are aware that marriage is a contract that automatically gives rights of inheritance to the spouse. At a time when we should be happy and celebrating a union, many older marriages cause controversy, upset and pain.

The remarkable thing is that both parties can avoid this scenario if they think the situation through sensitively. Decisions can be made and details organized (perhaps in the form of a prenuptial agreement) so that everything is clear. Accepting that problems may occur is often the first step towards finding a way forward. If all parties remain open and keep talking, a solution is usually possible whereby everyone's interests are preserved.

Pets

When people take on a pet they rarely think that it could outlive them. Animals can be a huge responsibility, and anyone who loved their pet would want it to be well looked after should anything happen to them. For many of us, a pet is more than just an animal; they are our friends and have a special place in our hearts.

Being a responsible pet owner is not just about feeding and exercising your pet. There can be significant veterinary bills, which tend to become larger and more frequent as the animal ages. This does not mean that you should decide not to take on a pet: pets are known to have calming and stress-reducing properties, to say nothing of the exercise you will get if you have to walk a dog. However, you should think forward to the future and leave a provision if you can.

Leaving a lump sum in the form of an insurance payment or even some savings in a separate account would enable someone to look after your pet in the manner to which they had become accustomed and ensure that they are cared for until the end of their days. It would also enable you to relax, knowing that your pet would be cared for in the event of being left without a home.

Decisions around money

Deciding what to do with your money and how to fund your retirement are hot topics these days. We are being moved away from expectations of inheritance as, increasingly, people have to sell their homes to provide for care in their later years.

Deciding to take out an insurance policy or release capital on your home is a big decision with implications for your family after you are gone. Unfortunately, many organizations (including reputable banks) are only too willing to provide money in return for property, but this will always be to their advantage and not yours – it is a business decision, after all. They are in the business of making money from their transactions and therefore you cannot expect them to offer a deal in your favour; however, neither do you want to be exploited.

This is not to say that you should not release some of the equity in your property if that is the most sensible action, but only that you should be careful when doing so, having considered all the implications.

Remember this: Take financial advice

You must take good, independent financial advice before signing any deal in respect of your savings or property. What sounds like a good deal now to help you out of an immediate fix might lead to serious problems later. Ideally, ask a relative or a solicitor to be present – they can oversee any transaction and give you honest advice so that you understand fully the implications of any deal.

Deciding to donate your organs

Organ donation, or leaving your body to science, is a highly sensitive topic and one on which we all have strong views. The important decision here is whether this is for you or not, and, if it is, you must declare it to the relevant organization, family and friends.

The decision to donate your organs or leave your body to research will mean that, should anything happen to you, someone will benefit after your death, and in many ways it is the ultimate gift from one person to another. However, the decision has to be a personal one and others in your family may not be sympathetic to your views, so you will need to explain the situation sensitively.

Communication is the key

This chapter has been all about decisions that we make (or could make) that have an impact after we have gone. This could of course be many decades away: you do not need to wait until you are over 60 before addressing these issues. However, they are serious decisions that can affect the way others remember us. It is sad but true that all our good deeds can be wiped out by problems or memories after we have passed on unless we try to explain our feelings to friends and family.

At the beginning of this chapter, I asked you how you would like to be remembered – what will come into the minds of others as they utter your name. That part of your life can be controlled to some extent, and you have the power to have a significant impact on this. However, the best way of ensuring that your wishes are carried out is to communicate them and explain why you want to take the action you have decided upon. Then everyone will be aware of your thoughts and why you want the actions you have chosen to happen.

Try it now

Think back through this section. These are all decisions that you can make now that will have an impact on others in the far future. Which ones are right for you? Make a note of any that you need to action in the next few weeks, and commit to discussing them with family and friends.

FOCUS POINTS

▶ By thinking ahead and making some plans for your legacy, family, friends and colleagues will understand and be able to implement your decisions.

▶ Make a will, even if you feel you do not have much to leave. It can be highly stressful for your family if you do not have one, and your possessions will not be distributed in the way you may have wanted.

▶ If you want to support a charitable cause both now and in the future, be specific and have a legal expert draw up the details, allowing for ongoing costs.

▶ Do not sign away money or property without proper legal advice.

▶ If you have pets, make sure there is sufficient provision for them should anything happen to you.

Chris is feeling much more settled now at Peters & Sons. He has made his decision to stay and his positive attitude and way of dealing with staff has resulted in a happy and productive atmosphere. He is surprised and flattered when Mr Peters calls him into his office and asks whether he is interested in buying into the business and becoming a co-owner. Chris knows that this is a huge decision and one that will affect his family, his whole future and beyond. He needs to research much more information before he can make such a major decision but he realizes that this would make him a business owner and, if he chooses this, he must not put his family in jeopardy if anything should happen to him or the business. He has a lot to think about but feels confident that he will make the right decision.

Pat understands that, now she has a business, she must think about changing her will to reflect this. Pat made a will many years earlier and realizes it is not up to date. Her house alone is worth much more now, and she would like specific people to have certain pieces of the jewellery she has acquired over the years. She also now has to make decisions about the disposal of her business, if she is not able to carry on at any point. She decides to go to a specialist solicitor as she now recognizes that she needs some professional advice and she does not want anyone to think badly of her after she is gone. With that aspect of her life sorted, she can now start building her business and look forward to a full and profitable future.

Next Step

Now that you have completed this book I hope you are feeling more confident about making decisions. You have learned that there is no one way of making decisions and that, to prevent them being misinterpreted, it is best to explain or communicate them fully if they are going to have an impact on other people. On the following pages are more resources you may find helpful.

Taking it further

Helpful websites

www.decisionmaking.org – for more information on decision making

www.businessballs.com – for more information and techniques on decision making

www.ehow.com – notes and examples of decision-making tools

www.decision-making-confidence.com – how to make a decision

Many psychology or management sites also have a section on decision making.

Further reading

Adair, J., *Decision Making and Problem Solving Strategies,* (Kogan Page, 2010) (also audio download)

Crawford, C., *Managers Guide to Mentoring* (McGraw-Hill Professional, 2009)

Ford, L., *The Guardian Guide to Volunteering* (Guardian Newspapers, 2007)

Gigerenzer, G., *Gut Feelings* (Penguin, 2008) (also audio book and Kindle)

Goleman, D., *Emotional Intelligence* (Bloomsbury Publishing, 1996)

Hammond, J., Keeney, R., and Raiffa, H., *Smart Choices* (HBS Press, 1999)

Harvard Business Review on Decision Making (Harvard Business School Press, 2001)

Jenner, P., *Teach Yourself Confidence and Social Skills* (Hodder, 2007)

Kourdi, J., *Decision Making* (Orion Business, 1999)

Kroqerus, M., *The Decision Book* (Profile Books, 2011)

Mannering, K., *Dealing with Difficult People Easily* (Hodder, 2011)

Michelli, D., *Teach Yourself Successful Assertiveness in a Week* (Hodder, 2012)

Pedler, P., *Action Learning for Managers* (Gower Publishing, 2008)

Russell-Jones, N., *The Decision Making Pocketbook* (Management Pocket Books, 2000)

Shapiro, M., *NLP Bullet Guide* (Hodder, 2011)

Steinhouse, R., *Brilliant Decision Making* (Pearson Education Limited, 2010)

Vickers, A., and Bavister, S., *Present with Impact and Confidence* (Teach Yourself, Hodder, 2010)

Contacts

International Association of Administrative Professionals – www.iaap-hq.org

Chartered Management Institute – www.managers.org.uk

Chartered Institute of Personnel and Development – www.cipd.co.uk

Institute of Administrative Management – www.instam.org

International Institute for Management Development – www.ism.edu

International Project Managers Association – www.ipma.ch

American Institute of Management – www.americaninstituteofmanagement.com

Project Management Institute – www.pmi.org

Voluntary Services Overseas (VSO) – www.vso.org.uk

Home and community volunteering – www.direct.gov.uk

Citizens Advice – www.citizensadvice.org.uk

Relate – www.relate.org.uk

Samaritans – www.samaritans.org

For learning programmes on decision making, contact your local college, adult education centre, or The Open University at www.open-university.co.uk.

Index

action learning sets, *31*
action, taking, *24–5*, *82–3*
analysis, *18–19*
appraisals, *95–6*
Asch, Solomon, *64–5*

blockers, *7–8*
body language, *17–18*
brainstorming, *35–7*
business decisions
    appraisals, *95–6*
    delegating, *97–8*
    importance of, *86–7*
    meetings, *90–1*
    negotiations, *91–2*
    operational, *89–90*
    recruitment, *93–4*
    staff development, *96–7*
    strategic, *87–8*
    teams, *92–3*
career breaks, *123–5*
career change, *121–2*
children, decisions with, *104–6*
connections, *4–6*, *32–3*
conscious decisions, *3–4*
consensus decision making, *74–5*
consequences, *80–1*, *129–38*
contingency funding, *49–50*, *52*
creative solutions, *19–20*
creativity, *28–39*
criteria, *22–3*, *38*, *73–4*
criticism, deflecting, *66–7*

decision blockers, *7–8*
decision-making process, *15–25*

defining problems, *8*
delegating, *97–8*
diet, *10*

education, selecting, *118–19*
ego preserving, *66–7*
elderly relatives, *122–3*
emotional decision making, *52*, *101–11*
emotional intelligence, *63–4*
emotional reactions, *8*, *17–18*
energy, need for, *9–10*
evaluation, *25*
exercise, *10*
expectancy effect, *106–7*

family decisions, *103–4*, *123*
fast decisions, *58–67*
financial decisions, *136–7*
Five Whys, *18–19*
focus groups, *75–6*
friends, *10*

game play, *64–5*
goals, *125–6*
grids, structured decision making, *76–8*
group decisions, *64–5*, *90–1*
group manipulation, *64–5*
guilt, *11*, *102–3*
'gut feelings', *62–3*

halo or horns effect, *108–9*
houses, decisions about, *119–21*

ideas, *29–32*
implications, *80–1*, *129–38*

instinct, *57*
intuition, *57, 62–3*

kinaesthetic strengths, *34–5*

leadership, *92*
legacies, *129–38*
life decisions, *114–26*
location decisions, *119–21*

marriage
    in later life, *135–6 see also*
        partners, choosing
meetings, *90–1*
memorials, *132–4*
modalities, *32–5*
money decisions, *136–7*
moral compasses, *65–6*
moving house, *119–21*
music, *34*

negative bias, *109–10*
negotiations, *91–2*

operational decisions, *89–90*
opportunities, using, *115–16*
options, *8, 29–30, 38*
ordering, *20–2*
organ donation, *137*
organization, of creative solutions, *20–2*
outcomes, *25*

partners, choosing, *117–18*
people
    engaging with, *23–4*
    and ideas, *31–2*
pets, *136*
plans, *23*

power differences, *110–11*
probability, of risk, *51–2*
procrastination, *58*
project-focused risk, *46–7*

questioning approach, *37*
quick decisions, *58–67*

recruitment, *93–4*
relatives
    elderly, *122–3*
    family decisions, *103–4*
retirement, funding, *136–7*
risk management, *42–53*
rollercoaster effect, *9*

safety-focused risk, *48–9*
schools, selecting, *118–19*
security-focused risk, *47–8*
selection, *22–3*
self-esteem, maintaining, *66–7*
sensitization, *116–17*
skills, *14–25, 75, 96–7*
sleep, *37–8*
staff development, *96–7*
stakeholder analysis, *81–2*
stereotyping, *107–8*
strategic decisions, *87–8*
structured decision making
    actions, *82–3*
    Christmas lunch example, *72–3*
    consensus, *74–5*
    consequences, *80–1*
    focus groups, *75–6*
    grids, *76–8*
    stakeholder analysis, *81–2*
    value of, *70–2*
    weighting options, *78–9*

teams, *92–3*
three pile strategy, *21*
time, for decision making, *6–7*
traffic light system, *51–2*

unconscious decisions, *3–4*
universities, selecting, *119*
unpopular decisions, *8*

visualization, *33–4*
volunteering, *131–2*

weighting options, *78–9*
wills, *134–5*
work change, *121– 2*

Notes

Notes